SAN FRANCISCO PUBLIC LIBRARY
3 1223 02540 0897

S0-DSF-105

The Bitter Taste of Glory

New York and Cleveland

The Bitter Taste of Glory

by JACK VALENTI

THE WORLD PUBLISHING COMPANY

ACKNOWLEDGMENTS

The author expresses his gratitude for permission to quote from the following works:

Randolph of Roanoke: A Political Fantastic, by Gerald Johnson, G. P. Putnam's Sons, New York.

John Randolph of Roanoke, by Russell Kirk, Henry Regnery Company, Chicago.

History of England, by Thomas B. Macaulay, G. P. Putnam's Sons, New York.

Great Contemporaries, by Winston Churchill, G. P. Putnam's Sons, New York.

A History of the English Speaking Peoples, by Winston Churchill, Dodd, Mead & Company, New York.

The Magnificent Century, by Thomas B. Costain, Doubleday & Company, New York.

The Story of Philosophy, The Age of Louis XIV, by Will Durant, Simon & Schuster, Inc., New York.

The Character of a Trimmer, by H. C. Foxcroft, Cambridge University Press, New York.

The Greek Way, by Edith Hamilton, W. W. Norton & Company, New York.

The Making of the President, 1968, by Theodore White, Atheneum Publishers, New York.

Francis Bacon: The Temper of a Man, by Catherine Drinker Bowen, Little, Brown & Company, Boston.

Disraeli, by Robert Blake, Eyre & Spottiswoode, Ltd., London.

Disraeli and His Day, by Sir William A. Fraser, Routledge & Kegan Paul, Ltd., London.

Disraeli: A Picture of the Victorian Age, by André Maurois, Hawthorne Books, New York.

Published by The World Publishing Company
Published simultaneously in Canada by Nelson, Foster & Scott Ltd.
First printing—1971

Library of Congress catalog card number: 78-145837
Printed in the United States of America

WORLD PUBLISHING
TIMES MIRROR

To:

Mary Margaret

Courtenay

John

Alexandra

Winston Churchill wrote of the death of Henry II: "... so saying, this hard, violent, brilliant and lonely man expired on July 6, 1189. The pious were taught to regard this melancholy end as the further chastisement of God upon the murderer of Thomas Becket. Such is the bitter taste of worldly power. Such are the correctives of glory."

Preface

I am not a professional historian nor do I pretend to be. I am an amateur scholar fascinated with politics, politicians, power and powerlessness, with extraordinary men and their collision with crisis and conflict, victory and defeat.

As a reader of history I am struck with the fact that the terribly difficult issues of today are not unique. They have a similarity to problems of other eras, when other leaders grappled with the same kind of torments.

After many years working in politics, from the precinct to the White House, I am impressed by the role of human nature in politics, the interaction of the human spirit in the deciding of the great issues. The human element, the personality and fragility of the political man, as well as his vitality and calm and instinct, are invested in every moment of decision. When the anatomy of political conflict is examined, human nature is as much present today as it was in the time of the Athenians. And human nature is pretty much the same in any century.

It occurred to me when I worked in the White House, as I read and re-read history to give myself some new insights that

I did not have before, that millions of young people now in school, wrestling with history and possibly bored and fretful, would find history more exciting if it could be tied to today, and made relevant to modern political life, and to the human element in the public man.

What I have attempted to do in this little volume is to speak to the young as I would have wished someone to speak to me when I was young, not talking down to me, but speaking straight about human beings who found themselves in positions of power and how they handled that power. If the reader wants something deeper or more revealing, he can go to the professional historian. I have really only touched the surface.

I hope that what is written here may find some hospitality within young people who are interested in or are studying the odd and formless experience we call political life. For if life is, as John Masefield described it, beauty chased by tragic laughter, then some of these recountings may be pertinent.

Let me be clear about what this book is and what it is not. It is not meant to be an in-depth search for everything in the lives of the men this book is about. It is not meant to be a detailed examination of all that these men did and aspired to. It does not reveal some new dimensions found in new, undiscovered material. It is none of these. It is written as a book for young people (and for that matter, not-so-young people, too) which tries to capsule the lives, achievements, and despairs of some unusual men into brief essays, and to fit what they did and did not do into a modern-day political setting. It is strange how much things change and how much they remain the same.

Throughout history there have been leaders, writers, philosophers, soldiers who bore the burdens of public apathy, loneliness, the response of a negligent public grown sour with them, or the curious cast of unhappy circumstances that shrouded their own great accomplishments in argument, critical outrage, and public disfavor.

Phocion of Athens determined to be honest in his appraisals

and wise in his judgments, seeking the peaceful way to the future though his countrymen shouted for war; and he was put to death when what he sought was ignored and what he feared was embraced.

Simon de Montfort put down the first foundations of a free society's governing apparatus; yet he died in violence, hated and feared not as a valiant precursor of a new kind of liberty but as an emerging despot.

Francis Bacon reached the pinnacle of power in Britain, a literary and political genius in an age in which there were some of each but few of both; and yet, when he was flying highest he was pulled down and destroyed.

Voltaire's pen scratched out with wit and venom the foibles of humankind, the absurdity of the clergy and his own peculiar prejudices, and he did it all with more craftsmanship than anyone before or since; yet he was hounded from his native land, doomed to perpetual exile.

John Randolph was the strangest light to illuminate the early days of the Republic, and the possessor of intellectual equipment that should have ordered a more productive life. But late in his life he was out of office, and during most of his life he was out of favor.

Disraeli overcame crushing handicaps of origin, appearance, and an empty purse to become the first minister of England and the Queen's devoted friend, all the while lavishing wit, irony, and satirical eloquence on friend and foe alike. Yet, after a lifetime spent in the pursuit of the highest office and having achieved it, he was thrown out, and his fiercest rival succeeded him.

George Savile, marquess of Halifax, served three English kings. A political moderate in an age of political turbulence and excess, Halifax's restraining influence shrank, until, when his wisdom was at its widest, he found himself beaten, frustrated, out of fashion and out of favor.

Thomas Babington Macaulay wrote the most eloquent history ever committed to English prose. But in the after-years of his work, he is the target of scorn and obloquy registered by critics who call his writing hopelessly baroque and his views maliciously biased.

In 1787, the Constitution of the United States was constructed during a hot Philadelphia summer by far-sighted men of good sense. Yet in the omission of a solution to slavery the men who made the Constitution lit the fuse that detonated the bloodiest war in American history, and nearly destroyed the nation they so ingeniously created.

Tragedy and conflict are part of the public man's travel kit. He knows they are there, sometimes unseen and sometimes distant, but always there, ready to materialize when they are least welcome, and always available to be whistled up by both enemy and unthinking friend.

The mythology of Greece and Rome is full of this *ambiance,* and indeed the four masters of dramatic tragedy of the stage (of whom three are Greek) used the theme of the leader beset by treachery and tragedy as the format for many of their plays. Trouble and challenge, success and defeat thus are ancient themes both in drama and in life.

All of these men in their own way tried, with varying degrees of success, to reform the society in which they were born, or about which they wrote, or to which they gave leadership. None was a nihilist or destroyer, and each attempted, in the frame of his own experience, to find the means to and give the inspiration for a social design that was better than the one he had found. Sometimes their own urgings were uncharted, welling up from some vast and sourceless instinct; sometimes what they chose to do or to describe had its roots in early moments of glory. They were all fascinating men, ranging from the possibly mad Randolph, to the irreverent Voltaire.

These are the men this book is about. Their common bond is politics, their writings about it, their participation in it, the ambitions they had for their country, the casualty of their unfinished business, the despair they suffered amid the triumphs they enjoyed. These men are dissimilar in almost every imaginable way, except in their encounter with the cruel mischiefs of Fate.

If this book has a generating force that caused it to be born, it is surely Norman Cousins. He is an unusual man. In my years of living in the political jungle, I have known a good many famous and actively concerned men and women. I have never encountered one whose dedication to what he believes is fastened so deeply in his conscience and in his heart as Norman Cousins'.

It was Cousins who encouraged me to write an article about Macaulay which was first published in the *Saturday Review*. Over the next year, four other articles of mine were published in the *Review*.

And now this book. There is still one more task to be done, and it must be done by others. It was E. M. Forster who said: "Books have to be read (worse luck, for it takes a long time); it is the only way of discovering what they contain. A few savage tribes eat them, but reading is the only method of assimilation revealed to the West."

We have deliberately made each of the following pages well-nigh indigestible to a vast majority of western and eastern stomachs, which, understandably, does limit one's choice of how best to absorb what is in them.

Washington, D.C. *Jack Valenti*
January 11, 1971

TABLE OF

CONTENTS

The Bitter Taste of Glory

phocion of athens:

A MAN FOR THIS SEASON

"Carpe diem" is an exhortation from Horace which means to seize the day, to grab opportunity when it appears. The young have attached themselves to this ancient counsel, and, besides the day, they are also seizing universities, induction centers, and peace candidates with audacity and undiminished fervor. These discontented, disaffected young have few heroes, and the ones they do have are those who tell it the way it is, tell it clean without varnish or adornment, tell it straight, and if this kind of telling is tough, then so be it, and three cheers for the teller.

Hidden away in the obscurity of another age is a man who could stand on any modern college rostrum and find in the young a mighty constituency. This philosopher-politician-soldier told it straight, except that he told it in Greece, a long time ago.

His name was Phocion, and he lived from about 400 B.C. to 317 B.C.

Plutarch said of him that his virtue was overmatched in the unequal contest with an adverse time, and that thus the ill fortunes of Greece brought him into history inglorious and unsought.

It is a matter of some debate whether the body politic enjoys the stern admonitions of a plain-spoken leader, who calls up for review the public voids, damns for all to hear the public vacancies, and tells the people what is best for them though his advice does not match the public mood. Some communities claim this virtue, but few nations ever give it substance. The leader who speaks in honest prose is seldom celebrated for his longevity in office.

The ancient philosophers had a bleaker eye than is commonly thought. Some of them, in an overview of the life and times of their leaders, found the public surly and inattentive when defeat and humiliation were the common bounty. Such times, said the philosophers, make the direction of public affairs a hazardous and none-too-attractive duty.

Phocion led Athens when Philip and Alexander prowled the ancient world, and none but the Macedonians found the future a thing of promise. Phocion was cynical about the hawks of his time, and, when Demosthenes was exhorting the people to crank up their machines of war against the Macedonians, it was Phocion who cautioned them against hasty action. It was Phocion who was not fooled by either the oratory or the guile of those who stood in the assembly and harangued the crowds with what he dismissed as a noisy charade. It is enough to say that in his eighties, Phocion, like Socrates, was condemned by the mob to drink hemlock, which he willingly did, for he was tired of telling the truth unheeded.

He rarely laughed or cried. He lived in the field like a common foot soldier. Indeed, those who served in battle under him were wont to smile and say that it was a very cold winter because Phocion was wearing a thin coat.

Once an Athenian leader chided him because of his solemnity, and when the people laughed at this jibe, Phocion remarked: "My sullenness never yet made any of you sad, but these men's jollities have brought you sorrow enough." The people stopped laughing.

He and Demosthenes were rivals in the public assembly. Demosthenes was the greatest orator of his generation, but it was also said that Phocion was the most powerful speaker. It was not how long he spoke, or the passion of his speech that found a response with the people, but a rare ability to compress in a few words what others would find necessary to expand to interminable lengths; an asset, it is to be claimed, cheerlessly lacking in this sophisticated and knowing twentieth-century generation. Once a friend found him behind the scenes of a theater where he was to address the citizenry, murmuring aloud to himself. "What are you doing, Phocion?" he was asked. He replied: "I am considering how I may shorten what I am going to say to the Athenians."

Chabrias, the Athenians' commander, sent Phocion to treat with an island from which Athens was demanding supplies. Chabrias wanted to send Phocion with an armed guard of twenty ships. Phocion said no, for if it were intended for him to approach the island as enemies, that force was insufficient, whereas if he were to regard them as allies and friends, one vessel was enough. He went with one vessel, offered friendship and affection to the magistrates, conveyed to them the trust that was in his heart, and returned with ships laden with the appropriate supplies.

Athens reached out for Phocion whenever the storm appeared, and the fact that he was elected general (a brazen piece of democratic action grown old-fashioned in later republics) on forty-five different occasions reflected the public respect for his integrity and wisdom, a respect, alas, which like so many public espousals wore thin in time, sundered by a faulty public memory.

It is part of Phocion's concept of leadership that he never was present at any of these elections, and refused to seek the generalship, contending that if the people wanted him, they would have to confer their favor without his regard.

He never drank the wine of applause, barely sipping it. He understood the fragility of fame. The people's momentary cheers never enlisted him in a fool's measure of the durability of public favor. He neither courted nor believed in that endurance. When the Delphic Oracle decreed that indeed Phocion was the ablest of Athenian leaders and advised his accession, it was Phocion alone who stood forward and disputed the Oracle's view, and when he presented himself thus to the people, they applauded and cheered him wildly. Turning to one of his friends, Phocion muttered, "Have I inadvertently said something foolish?"

After a war in which the people had been very timid and afraid, and which Phocion had brought to a close with neither great losses nor clear-cut victory, the people, regaining their confidence and bearing, bore down on Phocion, cursing him for denying them full triumph. In the midst of their uproar, Phocion retorted: "My friends, you are fortunate in having a leader who knows you, otherwise you would have long since been undone."

In a controversy with the Bœotians about some minor boundary dispute, he counseled negotiation. The other side blasted him, demanding war. "You had better," admonished Phocion, "carry on the contest with the weapons in which you excel, your tongues, and not by war, in which you are inferior."

Most of the well-known leaders opposed him, and none more severely than Demosthenes. The great orator scathingly addressed him one day, saying: "The Athenians, Phocion, will kill you some day when they are in a rage." To which Phocion dryly commented: "And you, Demosthenes, if they once again are in their senses."

Philip of Macedon was an ever-present danger. There came a time when it looked as if the Athenians, armed and roused, were ready to fight. At that precise moment, Philip showed signs of being tractable and peaceable, and Phocion counseled a treaty. One of his detractors denounced him, and demanded to know if he would persist in peacemaking now that the Athenians were confidently poised to do battle. "Yes," said Phocion, "I shall persist in the treaty though I know if there be war, I shall be in office over you, and if peace, you shall be in office over me."

Demosthenes' opinion carried the day, through his eloquently stated premise that it was better for Athens to make war as far away from home as possible, fighting the battle outside Attica.

"Good friend," said Phocion, "let us not ask where we shall fight, but how we may conquer in this war. That will be the way to keep it at a distance. If we are beaten, it will quickly be at our door."

After Philip's death, Alexander, then nearing the zenith of his sweep across the known world, wrote to Athens demanding a supply of vessels. Public speakers objected to sending them. Phocion, when asked his opinion by the council, advised acceptance. "Sirs," he said, "I would either have you victorious yourselves, or friends of those who are."

Another popular orator was Leosthenes, also a war hawk, who brought Athens into the Lamian war. He scoffed at Phocion's consistent hesitancy in unfurling battle banners, and scornfully asked Phocion what benefits he brought to the state after having been so many times elected general. "It is not a little," answered Phocion, "that the citizens have been buried in their own sepulchres and not on some battlefield."

And when Leosthenes continued to beseech the council, Phocion answered him: "Young man, your speeches are like cypress trees, stately and tall, and they bear no fruit."

He was assaulted by Hyperides in the assembly with the question, "When will the time come when Phocion will advise Athenians to make war?" Phocion replied: "As soon as I find the young men keep their ranks, the rich men contribute their money, and the orators leave off robbing the treasury." Hyperides, to coin a rich cliché, had no answer for that.

At a later time, when the people appeared eager to take the field against the Bœotians, he stood in opposition at first. His friends came to him and said to him that the people would kill him for always being in conflict with the majority view. "Ah," sighed Phocion, "that would be unjust of them if I give them honest advice; if not, it will be just of them." However, the majority view persisted and grew in volume, and against this overwhelming force of opinion, Phocion announced a proclamation that all Athenians under sixty should immediately outfit themselves with five days' provisions and follow him from the assembly into the field. This did cause some consternation among those older Athenians, and in their startled frenzy they cried out against the order. "Why do you resist?" shouted Phocion. "I am now four score and I am ready to lead you." The rage for war instantly subsided, as Phocion knew it would.

His view of citizens intruding on the business of command was both stern and emphatic. When a number of private citizens babbled to him about what hill he ought to occupy in the battle and how he ought to deploy his troops, an enduring public proclivity persisting to this hour, Phocion lifted his eyes to the sky and intoned: "Oh, Hercules, how many generals we have here, and how few soldiers."

On the forty-five separate occasions when Athens chose him for supreme command, he performed with valor and with rude disregard for the niceties of persuasion and flattery. Finally, in his eighty-fourth year, he failed to prevent the Macedonian seizure of Piraeus, and when the assembly took power again, they turned on this old man, full of years and larger honors than any other Athenian, and they put him to death for treason. More than that, they excluded his body from public burial, consigning it in fury to an oblivion which he did not deserve, but one from which he surely would never have cringed. His loyal wife gathered up his bones, dug a place for them by her fireside, and said: "Blessed hearth, to your custody I commit the remains of a good and brave man, and I beseech you, protect and restore them to the sepulchre of his fathers when the Athenians return to their right minds."

The political maxim to which Phocion gave proof is a simple one. The most precious asset a leader can have is believability. Eloquence, charisma, wit, beauty, all of these are of insubstantial worth compared to credibility, a faith in the leader's words and pledges. That is the nub of it all. When the dispassionate professional gauges the public merit of a rising leader, he puts the largest measure on believability, the most prized of electable traits. Does he instill trust in the people? Do they credit him with honest actions and redeemable words? Do they follow him because they know he tells the truth? Passion melts and fades. Emotion of a single day or week is an amorphous guide. The flash and fiery outbreak of an eloquent contagion has wider and sometimes more powerful appeal, but in the long run—and successful politics is metered in long runs—it is this valuable substance called believability on which political endurance must rest. All else shimmers and shines but has no solid bottom.

But being believable is more than a sincere expression, or the cast of one's jaw, or humble rhetoric. If the modern young have any assets, it is their ability to spot a phony. The art of the contrived, the plastic sculpting of make-up men, speechwriters, and secret counselors cannot hide, for long, the basic character of a man. Honesty is a very difficult trait to fake.

Phocion exhibited another trait that is found too seldom in most political leaders. It is the ability, and the courage, to admit mistakes. Strange, but most men who rise to high political station are not enchanted with the possibility of error, and even less attracted to the act of announcing it. In the tangled prism of human passions, and among those sourceless impositions of the mind that stir and beguile public men, there seems to be a genetic instinct that recoils from saying "I made a mistake" or "that was possibly not the correct move to make," or to admit publicly that a course of action taken might have been modified or revised.

To be believed the public man must produce in the people a disposition to believe him. To come by this formidable and precious asset the public man must not let what he says and does be disfigured by doubt or suspicion or the stern rebuttal of facts and truth. In short, he must say what he means and believes and do what he thinks is right. He must be honest, with the people and with himself.

Believability, then, is a combination of truth the public man speaks and honest action the public man takes, without fear of saying "I was wrong."

The people believed Phocion because in his long career of public service he never dissembled or conned them. They trusted him. But it is also true that a community or a nation can sometimes be as faithless as a leader. It was only when the Athenians lost their own good sense that they abandoned his.

The television camera has made the role of the leader, be he mayor, governor, senator, congressman, high cabinet official, or president, more open to public scrutiny. There is no handbook available to give instructions on how to install in the leader that sense of propriety and demeanor which makes his actions acceptable to the people. Charles de Gaulle, in his early book, *The Edge of the Sword,* set forth what the general deemed to be the public posture of an effective chief executive: "Nothing demonstrates authority better," said de Gaulle, "than silence. There can be no prestige without mystery for we have too little reverence for that which we know too well."

This may be true if the setting is right, that is, an environment and a society which places some value on memories and glory long since faded. But in this modern age what was once glory becomes counterfeit coin, with past grandeur now only shoddy reality, mottled with war and death and miseries, forgotten only because they are not present now.

Yet it is a bit disconcerting to search for the "why" of great leaders' hold on the people. When the historians rank the U. S. Presidents, they usually begin with Washington, Jefferson, Lincoln, Andrew Jackson, Woodrow Wilson, and Franklin Roosevelt. Is it significant that, with the exception of Jefferson, all of those chief executives lauded for their greatness achieved it in time of war? Perhaps it is because, as Lord Clark, the author of *Civilisation,* said on a television show, war brings the nation together in a unity that no other state of national excitement can. Great achievements are best nourished by national unity. The people close ranks during war, invest their leader with hopes for their own survival and victory, and are apt to see in the leaders' fulfillment of his duty a merit that in peacetime they would not find visible.

Indeed, one of La Rochefoucauld's memorable maxims says: "However dazzling an achievement may be it must not be accounted great unless it is the outcome of a great purpose."

One of the hardest tasks a modern leader has is to give to unglamourous, dreary, and difficult problems the garment of great purpose. How does the leader try to cleanse air and water, diminish poverty, lift the quality of living, enlist the nation in tolerance and understanding for those who are deprived, and clothe all these programs and objectives with the great sense of drama that war provides?

It is a quirky test of leadership, for these enterprises must be undertaken without the shield of a common enemy and the exaltation of those hopes which the possibility of battle ruin produces. Can the nation be brought together with that unifying passion bred by an attacking enemy when the enemy is ourselves, our neglect and our sponsored inequities?

Is there a lesson to be learned from Churchill, who having brought his island nation through its most terrible ordeal was flung from office once the blight had ended? Is there a corollary between de Gaulle, hustled offstage by the French in 1946 (to be frantically recalled twelve years later when the shattering of parliamentary government appeared to be lethal) and Phocion's fate?

In short, how does the modern society deal with mounting critical assaults on the leader, assaults made so much more open and swift (and more painful) by instant communication?

Moreover, it is plain that the leader will always be under attack from critics. In modern America instant communications have brought the President within critical mortar range of all the people. In an earlier age the White House was mostly shielded from the bludgeons because it was so difficult to communicate one's critical comments or opposing views. Today the notion, devised by some, that the President is isolated from the people, soundproofed against varying opinions and public displeasure, is a silly premise. In point of fact, the President is today more involved in the people's views than at any other time of our history.

The news, tons of it, good and bad, intrudes on the White House. It comes in bunches, on TV, radio, in newspapers, magazines, letters, visitors, all delivered to the President's residence or his office, or falls reluctantly, like wet confetti, from the lips of his aides and counselors. Then there are the hecklers and sign-bearers and picketers and just plain noise that tugs at him whenever he ventures beyond the South Grounds. And then there is the press, poking, thrusting, asking pointed questions, whose lances, the White House staff unanimously suggests, are tipped in curare. Even if the President is surrounded by the most loyal band of assistants, each pledged to the death to bring to the Boss only that which is cheerful or made to appear cheerful, the President is still bushwacked in one critical enfilade after another. Critics will find the President no matter how low his silhouette behind his aides or his office.

Some thoughtful observers, such as Washington journalist David Broder, have indicated their concern that in our zeal to set things right we are too rough with the President, whoever he is, and as a result we may be breaking the office and the man beyond reasonable repair. Are we as a nation so reducing the White House to rubble that we make it impossible for anyone to govern for any length of time? At any rate, it is a question that we ought to consider carefully before we give any answers.

And so, as it always happens, as it happened in Athens a long time ago, the society that flings a noble leader from his office in a fit of rage finds the mischief it has inherited, and the new leaders it has installed serve only to illuminate the memory of the gains it can no longer retrieve. People find the loss a void they have no force to fill. When finally the Athenians understood what happened, they repented. They put Phocion's accusers to death. They built a great brass statue of Phocion, and they reburied his bones in a grand ceremony. Then they mourned him, caused eulogies to be read, and wished anxiously that he would be present to guide them, for there were more storms and this time Phocion was not there.

It is all there in Plutarch, and the young, who fret for the lack of such a man, ought to read about him.

Simon de Montfort:

DARK FORCE? BRAVE VOICE?

Few men have come into the twentieth century from Plantagenet England the subject of more conflicting judgments than a remarkable and magnetic man named Simon de Montfort.

So unusual is the man himself that just that measure alone might suffice to give him space in history; but it is a singular accomplishment of his about which historians have loudly contended that affords him space in the history books. In the view of many, and not in the view of just as many more, Simon de Montfort was the father of the British House of Commons.

Simon de Montfort lived and died in violence. He was an arrogant, talented, stubborn, prideful man, the finest soldier of his day, an intimate of the most intelligent churchmen of that era, and a surly subject to his king, who was also his brother-in-law.

He surfaced in history on the edge of Plantagenet glory, in the reign of Henry III, who was the son of John, grandson of Henry II, and father of the first Edward. The times were in the thirteenth century, a bloody, coarse, and splendid environment when the political rostrum of England was being built. This rostrum would last for a thousand and more years not only in that island kingdom but also as a model of political architecture whose influence would change the governmental theme of Western Europe and would indeed cross an ocean to find residence in the New World.

A Norman by birth, Simon de Montfort came to England in 1229 to attach himself to the de Montfort claims on the lands and earldom of Leicester. It was a naive thing to do; though young and handsome he was penniless and unknown, while the estates of Leicester were firmly guided by the powerful noble Ranulf of Chester. Hopeless indeed was the verdict of his contemporaries: de Montfort is a fool, they said—attractive, yes, but a fool.

But immediately after Simon landed in England, Henry III took a fancy to him and brought him into the royal circle where the de Montfort charm gleamed and entreated all those in the court.

Simon was with Henry when the monarch descended on the coast of Brittany, an expedition of armor and madness doomed to a colossal failure. Henry returned to England bloodily defeated but as usual without any self-chastisement for a stupid and unnecessary venture. Henry found defeat a ready companion though not a congenial one.

But it was on the Brittany invasion that Simon ascended to those heights where only extraordinary charmers (or confidence men) reside; he convinced the aging Ranulf it was an act of decency and justice to convey the Leicester estates to de Montfort.

For whatever reason, the ceding of the Leicester lands to young Simon a short two years after his arrival in England was the thrust he needed. Now he was a peer, although a poverty-stricken one, possessing in spacious degree the manors and the manners of the high-born and the favored.

In the order of the times, the possession of large estates was both boon and bane. It took a considerable amount of money to maintain the large staffs so necessary to the endurance of royal favor and the legitimacy of feudal power. The way to this comfort, to a newly minted noble like Simon, was marriage to an heiress. He paid court to several. But a curious and fateful thing happened to Simon on his way to solvency; he fell in love, was rewarded by an ardent response, and was married (happily, fate chose, for the rest of his life) to Eleanor, sister to the King.

What appears to the viewer at this juncture of Simon's life is the picture of a man immersed in luck and good fortune, whose climb to power and fame is accompanied by success at every level. But in the minds of some of his friends there was a feeling that de Montfort was an arrogant adventurer, whose claims to achievement were neither valid nor honest.

However, Simon was more than his critics counted. Envy has a nasty habit of coloring judgment and obscuring talent. Already he became close to the noblest minds and boldest spirits of the age. One friend was Robert Grosseteste, the greatest churchman of the time. He was the most penetrating thinker of his time. So clear was his ability he stood pre-eminent among the eminent. Grosseteste recognized in de Montfort the steel behind the shrine, the depths beyond the shallows. Through Grosseteste, de Montfort drew closer to Adam Marsh and other formidable churchmen. De Montfort was privy to a wide-ranging learning flowing from the thoughts and conversation of the most distinguished single group of scholars in the kingdom.

Through the next years, the relations between the King and his brother-in-law were a mingling of disaffection, outrage, awe, and perhaps a little fear—not Simon of the King but vice versa.

There was an excursion in Gascony where Simon was dispatched by Henry to ride down and quell a guerrilla rebellion among the fractious Gascons. Simon fell upon Gascony with a harsh, brutal hand, and the Gascons felt a severity of justice they had never received from earlier England overlords. Later, de Montfort returned to England, and shortly after, the Gascons, relieved of stern disciplines, stirred again to insurrection. Simon learned of this while in Paris, and wrote the King a letter which is important in the probing of the later Simon. It is the only known writing of de Montfort that historians tell us is in existence. It is also the first visible evidence (to the King) of an alarming notion and turn in Simon's mind about law and government and the nebulous rights of the average man. One phrase deserves to be mentioned: ". . . because I uphold against them your rights and those of the common people. . . ." Simon was writing about the marauding Gascons, but it was a strange use of a strange phrase, "the common people," compelling because it touched upon a nerve edge so recently exposed, this damnable idea that rights resided in the lower classes. In 1250, this was a wild effrontery, a ridiculous whim whose lunacy would not be lost on Henry, too recently the grandson of Henry II who booted and spurred an entire Europe to his will, and too painfully the son of John who was forced by a band of rowdy barons to sign that devilish document called Magna Carta.

Had Henry been more prescient than stubborn, he might have sensed a spark of innovation in his brother-in-law which might be better dealt with at the end of a broadsword.

But Henry's sensitivity was dulled by a carapace of kingly divinity that insulated him from ideas, those which could have helped him as well as those which almost did him in.

Thereupon Henry indulged himself in a series of blunders which must be recorded as being so stupid and unfeeling that only a monarch serenely confident of some sort of divine installation would have been the designer of what might be charitably described as continual error.

The King allowed free rein to his Lusigan half brothers. They were a pair of freebooters who truly believed that all those not of royal blood counted not a fig and displayed this arrogance with all the coarse violence that they could summon. The three of them stomped about the kingdom fetching up revenues to pay for ventures like the Sicilian caper, in which Henry attempted to put his son on a shaky, bankrupt throne. The King came out of it with an empty pocketbook and sorely wounded pride.

Suffice it to say that the powerful barons resented this, and amid their grousing determined to do something about it.

There took place on April 9, 1258, what is known as the

Hocktide Parliament. It began inauspiciously, but it was fueled by a stirring of discontent that grew larger every day because of the weakness and the profligacy of the King.

An open confrontation occurred, an ugly scene where armed barons, furious and vexed, frightened the King and caused him to consider further their demands for a more suitable and less stringent rule. Later that summer, at Oxford, there were hammered out what are called the Provisions of Oxford, the work of de Montfort (though he was physically abroad on the Continent) and his rough and ready colleagues.

For the first time, an English sovereign agreed to two new bodies, the first a council of fifteen men who would sit continuously with the King and counsel him; the other a group of twenty-four to oversee the problems of the kingdom and to determine ways to solve them. The meaning of the Provisions of Oxford was clear: there was a veto power over the King, a veto over his actions and his plans, and there was a brake and a rein put to the hitherto unbounded menace of royal caprice. Henry naturally hated to sign, but he did. At that moment, Simon de Montfort, just under fifty, was the most powerful landed lord in England. There is no full evidence that his head was crowded with egalitarian notions, or that he had a precise plan of action which would lead to any permanent arena of freedom for the people. De Montfort was handsome, strong, and fearless, capable of a concentrated fury, and his blood contained rash passion even as through it flowed undefined purposes, perhaps a puzzle to himself. His marriage was sure, and so was his hold on his fellows.

The King's advisers, Machiavellian before the word was invented, gathered his attention and caused him to be absent from England so that the next Parliament would not be called and the hated Provisions be null and void. When Simon declared himself in favor of convening the Parliament with or without the King, Henry hastily returned to England and imperiously canceled the Provisions. By his side was the long-shanked

Plantagenet youth who was his son and one day to become Edward I. It was this young prince, now moving into maturity and more certain of his strength and his cause, who determined that the barons had gone too far. Civil war, young Edward concluded, would come—and let it come, for the barons must be punished.

Simon knew, too, that the time for armed action was at hand. For a time before the King denounced the Provisions, Simon and his fellow barons were at an uneasy fork in the road, grumbling among themselves. But when the sovereign trampled the Provisions, the surly lords shed their own vexations, looked to Simon for leadership, and the gauntlet so long waved precariously in the air was flung down.

Both armed forces deployed in the field. Because the King had the superiority of numbers, the royal army moved eagerly to battle. At Lewes, on the road leading from the channel ports to London, the storm of fire and blood exploded. Simon with daring and a shrewd sense of timing deceived Henry's men, out-generaled the young Edward who was tasting for the first time, but not the last, the sour, sweet gourd of battle, sealed all escape routes, and butchered the King's men. Both Henry and Edward were ingloriously captured. Simon was in charge of England.

In 1265, de Montfort assembled in London a Parliament unlike any called before, and in whose wake grew an English apparatus for public expression, shaped and nurtured by what this Parliament meant and symbolized. Simon summoned peers, bishops, two knights for each shire, and from two to four loyal men from each city and borough. The significance to an emerging England was profound. For the first time plain, ordinary citizens rubbed parliamentary elbows with the high-born and the powerful. Moreover, they were called to action and convened without the consent and even the presence of the King.

Thus was exhibited for the first time in history an instrument of participatory involvement in the government in which common men and peers met simultaneously. With this display there was the novel idea that the public instrument could function in the ruler's absence and indeed in the face of his express prohibition.

This was called the Great Parliament, not for its achievements but because of the towering precedent it built for ages to follow.

Authority to run the state was centered in a triumvirate; Simon, the volatile Gilbert, earl of Gloucester, and Stephen Birkstead, the bishop of Chichester. The loose and wearied arm of the government grew tighter and stronger under this group, though it became clear that Simon was the first among equals. If he had any misgivings about loosing his fierce energy (which others grumbled was an avaricious ambition), they did not deter him or stay his firm and competent hand. He immediately brought order to a disordered land, initiated reforms, traveled tirelessly throughout the kingdom, and did it all with his peculiar and dominating zeal.

Yet his was a curious position. He was the leader of the opposition, the brother-in-law of the King, but he was denied access to the throne. To oppose is one thing, but to be able to achieve final, definable power is another. There was reason and right on his side, but no legitimacy. To an emerging English state, the mystic glory of the Plantagenet dynasty was still ample, and de Montfort, for all his soldierly abilities and vast baronial strength, was still a foreign usurper. Thus, the tragedy of de Montfort and his strivings for order in the land was hung up on the fixed truth of heredity and the blood claims of Henry and Edward.

While power and royal authority are interchangeable when wielded by kings, it was de Montfort's dreary fate that he had the ability to exercise the one but no chance to attain the other.

Moreover, he was not without error, both in the speed with which he accumulated estates, and in his failure to hold fast to the loyalties and affections of the mercurial Gloucester. This moody man, of uncertain and passionate temper, grew morose and fell out with Simon. It was the ageless story of a proud man who believed himself to be left out of decision making, with no due given him for his rank and position. Though Simon could appropriately answer there were hard duties to perform, and a country to govern with little time to soothe and placate ruffled ducal feelings, it was not enough to satisfy Gloucester. It is plain that princes and presidents, to their bitter regret, always learn that pouring balm over the ego of outraged allies and coadjutors of power is a necessary, even obligatory, task, as vital as the public business itself. When Gloucester later made visible his souring rage, Simon's absence of sensitivity to the personal pride of the earl turned into a fatal blunder.

And so the noose tightened. The more Simon struggled to extend his dominion over the nation which needed competency, for too long vacant, the more impermanent his own tenure seemed. The royal hemp pressed him more helplessly against events over which he lost the power to control.

When Edward escaped his laxly guarded confinement, it became clear that Simon's political illegitimacy was too high a barrier to surmount. Edward courted Gloucester, still sulking, persuaded him to join the royal forces, and having done so, the young prince aroused other nobles, grown vexed with Simon's no-nonsense leadership and his insistence on order and efficiency. De Montfort's boot was heavy, and its imprint was increasingly felt on the necks and boundaries of the barons. His own assumption of so much of the power apparatus began to rupture the bonds binding him to his peers, and enlarged the suspicion that Simon was nourishing odd notions of becoming a dictator. The war, so recently won, began again.

Simon at the head of his army marched from Hereford, crossed the Severn at Kempsey, four miles north of Worcester. Then he proceeded to the Abbey of Evesham, where he camped, and waited for the army of his son Simon to join him for the assault on Edward. He did not know that the young Simon would never arrive, for his son's dalliance and foolishness en route allowed Edward to surprise him and cut his troops to bits.

On August 4, 1265, the battle of Evesham began. A little over a year after de Montfort had mounted a successful rebellion against the ineptness of an erratic king, he was overrun by Edward. He watched his other son, Henry, cut down before his eyes. With his customary courage he fought until he was alone, sword in hand, and, wounded, friends and foes clustered around him, fought until a vicious broadax blow brought him down. Not satisfied with his death, the royal warriors hacked him into pieces, his arms, legs, and head exhibited in public places. It was an ugly end for the largest leader of his day.

After his death, there was a strange resurgence of belief in Simon among the common people, and miracles were attributed to him, an eerie echo of another death and other ascribed miracles when Thomas à Becket was murdered in his cathedral.

Both the miracles and the man have been savagely debated ever since. Whether or not popular government in England endowed itself in that first Great Parliament authored by de Montfort is a prime question, but there are other questions which in the asking have meaning for today's generation.

Where the historians collide is not so much on the value of the precedent of the Great Parliament, but in the fascinating summary of just what de Montfort had in mind.

Was he specifically delivering what he had written in that still-existent letter to the King, wherein he proclaimed the rights of the common man, or was he an incipient dictator, glorying in the craving for absolute power? It is this curious search for the personal man which tortures and enlivens historical debate. To take a man's measure is the sport of the historian. In a cynical moment, Lord Acton once observed that there are no unselfish patriots. Every man in public life works for his own end. But the statesmen whom history respects are those who identified themselves with noble instead of base aspirations. Hitler became the focal point of everything that was ignoble, whereas Churchill became the spokesman of his country at its moment of highest courage.

Simon's struggle, then, becomes the model for the endless

conflict between the glories of liberty and the tyranny of despotism.

Yet how is one really to judge? Could Simon's early opposition to the King have sprung from a frustrated ambition, and then later redeployed into an inspired regard for the public good?

There were in his possession all the talents and the weapons of the demagogue and the statesman; proud, brave, capable of sustaining an inspired loyalty, he was able to influence and overwhelm both followers and rivals, and seed within himself the rich righteousness so invulnerable to enemies and so shiningly attractive to friends.

However, the dangers of dark forces in a man like Simon were catalogued by Sir Robert Cotton almost four hundred years after Simon's death. In writing about de Montfort, Cotton said that the perils were in the starting of a train of events which would end disastrously. "We must be aware," he wrote, "of running down steep hills with weighty bodies. Once they are in motion stops are not then voluntary."

Sir Robert's grave warning is apt, but it is not new. Polybius gave us a condensed version of Thucydides' basic theory about power. Human power, he said, is a cycle in which excess of power keeps revolving. The more power one has, the more he wants, and he goes on abusing his authority until an inevitable opposition arises and a few men, strong enough when they unite, seize the rule for themselves. They, too, can never be satisfied. They intrude on the rights of others until they are opposed in turn. The people are aroused against them, and democracy succeeds to oligarchy. But then again the evil in power is no less operative. It brings corruption and contempt for the law until the state can no longer function and falls easily before a strong man who promises to restore order. The rule of the one, recalls Polybius, of the few, of the many, each is destroyed because there is in them all an unvarying evil—the greed for power—and no moral quality is necessarily bound up with any of them.

The people, said Plato, have always some champion whom they set over themselves and nurse into greatness. This and no other is the root from which a tyrant springs; when he first appears he is a protector.

It is this collision of desires which causes political anguish: the craving for power on the part of the leader and the reach for a stable society on the part of the public, for the latter fetches the former, alien though they appear to be.

It is no less true in our time that it was in Simon's. Thucydides' concept is as imperishable as it is ancient. Power begets the passion for more power, or at least the preservation of power. My hunger for power, says Marguerite Yourcenar, quoting Hadrian, is like the craving for love which keeps the lover from eating or sleeping, from thinking or even from loving as long as certain rites remain unperformed.

The visible truth of our times is the simple axiom that every man in public office has an enlarged ego and that the response of the public is his opiate, needed, defined, and indispensable. There are some officials who will deny this, and demand to be believed that theirs is a cause, a crusade, pure, untarnished, isolated from ambition. This is not entirely untrue, but usually at the base of every personal political pinnacle is the desire for glory, for applause, for power. This is as true among radical revolutionaries as it is among political "straights."

What the citizen does not often choose to understand, and what pious pundits insist on making invisible, is the easy camaraderie between good and bad. Ofttimes, as Lord Acton so frankly described, the public good and the private gain are intermingled, and the nation benefits.

If Simon appropriated both power and estates, he equally lavished order and justice (of a kind) on the countryside. If his aim was to embrace within his own person the ultimate authority of the state, he was also determined to bring to an aimless and feckless national community the stability for which it longed. If he can be criticized for his appetite for authority, may he not also be praised for his innovative Great Parliament, which, for the first time, purified the political air? Was he dark force or brave voice? This is an elemental political question forcing answers from an uneasy public as relevant in the twentieth century as it was in the thirteenth.

It may be that the United States has fashioned a weaponry which allows this intermingling to take place but within prescribed limits. This weapon is the dispersal of final authority through the complex checks and balances of a finely flexible Constitution, plus a most sensible barrier to more than two terms in the presidency. Some political scientists believe a six-year presidential term without re-election is an even more effective device. The President could act on every issue without any thought of its impact on his re-election campaign. He would have no re-election campaign. The changing of the guard is a constitutional detergent. It washes away centers of power that crust on the bureaucracy. Impermanence always waits outside the door of the American leader in the White House, and it is this lack of tenure that intrudes every time he attempts to harden his resources and lengthen his reach.

But if we in this country—and indeed peoples in other civilized establishments in the world—like to indulge ourselves with the notion that our leaders have no urgings other than to lead, without applause or public love or the rosy accompaniment of the perquisites of power, then let us indulge ourselves. But let us also recall that no man freely enters the public arena, a cheerless landscape at best, endures both calumny and indifference, and accepts his unsheltered lot with as much composure as he can summon, unless there resides within him the power dazzle which flames in almost every public man. There is nothing wrong in this. That a leader is vain is no indicator of his worth or lack of it. Indeed, it may be said that only egocentric men have the resolution and energy to lead successfully.

A moment of terror or doubt, when a fixed decision needs to be made, is not a time for reluctance or modesty or the murmured thought that a committee ought to decide. What is needed then is a grand conceit that serves the leader and gives him the propulsion to face the monster and strike him down with a calm, clearly called decision. His decision may not be a good one, but inaction or paralysis sometimes can be worse. But then it is highly unlikely that a shrinking violet would ever brave the political swamps that surround the White House or any other high elective office.

De Gaulle had a rather imperial sense about the authority of the leader (see his comment about qualities of a leader in the chapter on Phocion). De Gaulle summed up the role of a private arrogance in the public man when he defined how decisions are made: "The assemblies debate, the ministers govern, the constitutional council thinks, the President of the Republic decides."

It is hard to conceive any man wanting to be President who would turn away from that definition of decision-making.

All of this is not to be unaware of another shaping force that invites a man into public service. It is the need to do something beyond the ordinary selections of a life. The sure feeling that a man is making a contribution to the advance of his country or state or city, something beyond the petty grubbing for material things, is a powerful incitement.

The dimensions of this force vary from man to man. It is difficult to measure precisely. But it is there and it can be large. It is present in most great democratic leaders and even in lesser men serving in lesser offices it is a powerful thrust.

To many thoughtful observers, a public man's achievements are in direct proportion to this sense of public duty he has within him. There is no pulse of action that beats more steadily than the feeling in the public man's gut and heart of honestly caring about what happens to the people he has sworn to serve.

This concern which fixes itself deep inside the public man's conscience is the generator of zeal and purpose that will not be turned aside by opposition or frustrating events.

It is this curious mix of the power-dazzle and a sense of service that beckons to the ambitious man of energy, and causes him to plunge into the political forest, sometimes without a map or a compass. It probably was no less the same adventure and mingle of passions in the 13th century as it is now.

In an antique world, Simon was the forerunner of the modern political leader. His progeny are everywhere today.

But the pace is swift and terrible, and the public man, driven by his own urgings, has no steady reference point. He can go down as quickly as he went up, or fall abruptly no matter how long he lingered on the top. Sophocles might have had the public official in mind when he wrote his ageless, grieving lines:

> the long days store up many things nearer to grief than joy
> . . . and last of all, old age, despised, infirm, unfriended.

But, Edith Hamilton points out, "to men like Sophocles outside change does not bring the loss of inner steadfastness. The strong can keep the transient and the eternal separate."

It is a discipline to be learned by societies as well.

Francis Bacon:

THE GLORY AND THE SHAME

He was a writer, a philosopher, a scientist, a jurist, a high government official, a politician. He came from a family long immersed in state business. His father had held the highest office in the land. He was superbly educated, became a lawyer, a member of Parliament, was appointed Queen's Counsel, ascended higher—though slowly—in the councils of the court to Solicitor General, Attorney General, and, at the age of fifty-seven, to a summit of power as Lord Chancellor. He was knighted and named Baron Verulam and Viscount St. Albans.

All the while, he roamed the vast and largely uncharted field of the mind, in both science and philosophy, and wrote what is today the most preciously valued book of essays in all English-language literature. Then, while he dwelt on the heights, he fell from power into disgrace—an awful, sordid, tormented fall—hooted out of office by his enemies, none with his genius but all armed with more vengeance and guile than he knew they had. He was dead a few years later.

This was, of course, Francis Bacon—sternly judged by some, exalted by most. Macaulay described Bacon as being inhabited with "all the powers of the most exquisitely constructed intellect that has ever been bestowed on any of the children of men."

Francis Bacon is immensely human. He is full of all the paradoxes and yearnings and fits of depression that afflict most of us. There is something sad in seeing this extraordinary man grubbing for a royal smile, whining to his powerful uncle, William Cecil (Lord Burghley), for a job. Bacon, like many a modern man, believed that he was fit for larger things, and he ached to show his mettle. Moreover, he was not above using what influence he could, or subtly putting the shaft to those who crowded the path he chose to follow.

Bacon hitched his wagon to a shooting star. His luck was bad, for the star rose in a blazing trajectory that, unhappily for Bacon, curved too sharply and fell on an executioner's ax. Robert Devereux, the second Earl of Essex, dashing, arrogant, foolish, made his run for power, thoughtless of Queen Elizabeth's inner edge of steel, and was put to death. Bacon, who had courted him and counseled him, and secretly planned to rise to supreme power with him, was now isolated.

During all those years, Bacon had waited for the Queen's favor. Elizabeth was conscious of Bacon's immense gifts. He had some influence on her, particularly in the logic that he employed to persuade her in matters of state, logic garmented in the aphoristic eloquence which Bacon alone was capable of conceiving.

Before Essex's execution, the Queen, vexed at a pamphlet she had read which had been dedicated to Essex, called Bacon to a hearing before the Lord Chancellor. The pamphlet was seditious, at least so the Queen complained.

"Do you see treason in it?" the Queen asked Bacon.

"Madam," answered Bacon, "you may punish the author not for treason, but for felony. He has stolen most of his passages from Tacitus."

As often happens in a kingdom, a republic, or a township, men grapple for favor and power. Bacon engaged in a lifelong struggle with his greatest and severest rival, the most famous jurist of the century, Sir Edward Coke. In some strange, almost occult manner, Coke managed to best Bacon in every contest. With each setback, Bacon's irritation for Coke turned more savage, yet he seemed hopelessly consigned to second place. Coke rose to

Attorney General, to which Bacon had for so long aspired. Bacon raged.

They collided in open court.

Catherine Drinker Bowen describes the confrontation:

> "Mr. Bacon," said Coke, "if you have any tooth against me, pluck it out, for it will do you more hurt than all the teeth in your head will do you good."
>
> "Mr. Attorney," shouted Bacon, "I respect you, I fear you not, and the less you speak of your greatness, the more I will think of it."
>
> "I think scorn," replied Coke curtly, "to stand upon terms of greatness toward you, who are less than little, less than the least."
>
> Bacon answered: "Mr. Attorney! Do not depress me so far. For I have been your better and may be so again, when it pleases the Queen."

It never pleased the Queen. When she died in 1603, a reigning monarch for nearly forty-five years, Bacon was still just a Queen's Counsel, a far place from the heights to which all his longings were directed. James I became the king of England. Though Bacon was not to know it on that day of James' accession, the road to power was to open splendidly to his view and journey. Within the next eighteen years, he was to experience the relish and the zest of success in politics.

He was also to begin his writings, which in the perverse logic of history, were to provide him with a platform destined to stand long after his political power had blown away.

In 1597, six years before the death of Elizabeth, the first Bacon essays appeared. The second volume was published in 1612, and a third in 1625.

Bacon designed a difficult form of prose. The sentences divide like a carpenter's rule into instantly recallable maxims. This succinct style, so demanding of unerring craftsmanship, is what makes Bacon's essays so readable today.

It was in these years that Bacon's life design became relevant.

He had lived too long in penury, and as he stood poised on the periphery of the court and the courtables, he found the aroma of the good life pleasant, and he knew that it was available to those whose purse and power were fat. He panted after both.

Later, when he assumed the trappings as well as the fact of power, he revealed part of himself to the Spanish ambassador, a crafty, sensitive, Machiavellian artisan of the diplomatic game. Ah, Bacon told the ambassador, while he was burdened with all the symbols and the duties of supreme leadership, he really would rather live a simple private life.

> The wise old ambassador smiled politely. Yes, he replied thoughtfully, he certainly understood this human longing of Lord Bacon. "Would the good Lord Bacon permit him to recount an ancient Spanish fable?"
>
> "Of course," Bacon responded.
>
> "Very well, then," said the ambassador. "An old rat, it seemed, told all the young rats that he wanted to leave the world and retire. He would go into his hole and spend his time in contemplation and would renounce all pleasures for he was tired of the empty splendid life he had led. He commanded the young rats not to come to visit him, indeed, to leave him be in his retirement. The young rats agreed, but after two or three days, they grew restless, for they wanted to see their leader, and to view him in his simple, spartan retirement. After all, they reasoned, he might be sick or even dead. They quietly entered the hole, and there they found the old rat sitting in the middle of a rich Parmesan cheese."

A shadow dogs Bacon's footsteps through history's pages. When there was a choice to be made between what he thought to be a new pathway to success or loyalty to the one man, Lord Essex, who had been his steadfast friend, he may have hesitated a bit (though the facts disfigure this notion), but he turned his back on the friend—indeed, he rose to testify in print against him. Then he torpedoed Coke, drove him from the chief justiceship, and unknowingly sowed the seed for his own destruction, for Coke's memory—like his patience—was long and implacable.

Consider Francis Bacon in February, 1621. He was the most brilliant public man in the island kingdom, now risen to Lord Chancellor of England, the trusted chief adviser of James I. Furthermore, he had served in the Commons and knew more about government and its course than any other man. Wise, knowledgeable, magnetic, full of confidence and skill, he bestrode the new Parliament, now convened, the first in seven years.

Three months later, he was ruined.

Coke had returned to Parliament, and with him sat a group of tough, able parliamentarians—Finch, Pym, Alford, Hakewill, Noye—determined to be heard and ready to destroy George Villiers, the King's favorite, who, as the marquess of Buckingham, lavished favors and power on his friends, among whom was Francis Bacon, the Lord Chancellor. The stage was ready, the cast was set, the curtain went up, and, by a quirk of fate and circumstance, Bacon became the villain.

The Parliament began by trying to reform a portion of the King's governing apparatus. The first to gain Parliament's attention were the monopolies—feasty plums bestowed on friends of the King, from which one could become very rich indeed. Bacon stood aloof, though his two brothers were involved as monopoly referees—another bit of largesse which paid much tribute. Then a second attack was made, and this, though appearing harmless, was the deadlier of the two. It was the work of the Committee for Inquiring into Abuses in the Courts of Justice.

As is usually the case when a conflict occurs, it emerges from some slight and obscure beginning, carelessly ignored at the time, yet, like a cancer, it quietly, lethally grows and destroys. In this instance, a man named Cranfield, slighted by Bacon and resentful of the Chancellor's arrogance, and a man named Churchill, a minor clerk who confessed to forging orders and who cried out that he would not fall alone but would carry others with him, were the two principal actors in a sordid scene—actors who would have their day and their say and then vanish from history only to be remembered because of their association with genius.

The committee learned from Cranfield that Chancery (the courts over which Bacon presided) was sheltering debtors, intimating that this was done for a price. Other complaints followed. On March 14, 1621, Sir Robert Phillips, chairman of the committee, reported that great abuses had been uncovered. "The person against whom these things are alleged," he concluded, "is no less than the Lord Chancellor." A man named Aubrey had a case pending in Chancery. He received a hint from Sir George Hastings, a member of Bacon's household, that a present of one hundred pounds would expedite matters. He gave the money to Bacon, and the Lord Chancellor accepted it. Later, Aubrey was pained to learn that he had lost his case.

Another complainant, named Egerton, said that he had been induced by two of the Chancellor's house guards to make a present to Bacon of four hundred pounds in gold, as "a thankful remembrance from a client, designed to buy a new set of hangings for York House." According to witnesses, Bacon was given the money, seemed surprised, and said it was too much money for the "gift" it was intended to be. Instead of returning it, however, Bacon laid it carelessly on one of his chairs. Nonetheless, after making the gift, Egerton lost his case.

The debate raged in the Commons and in the committee. It was a gift to Bacon, shouted his partisans, and what is wrong with that? It was a bribe, insisted Coke and his adherents, and that is very wrong. Bacon thus far was not under indictment, but he sniffed the air and found it foul. Slowly, inexorably, events closed in on Bacon, the footfalls making no echo, the closing doors no sound. He wrote to Buckingham: "I know I have clean hands and a clean heart, and I hope a clean house for friends and servants. But" (and here he got to the heart of practical political matters) ". . . [things] may for a time seem foul, specially in a time when greatness is the mark and accusation is the game." To the King, Bacon wrote prophetically: "Those who now strike at the Chancellor will soon strike at the crown. I am the first sacrifice. I wish I may be the last."

Bacon knew that the charge overwhelms the reply. The tiniest of indictments can bring a great man down. Moreover, for the first time, he seemed a bit bewildered. Didn't every man in high office accept gifts? Indeed, James I told the Venetian ambassador: "If I were to imitate the conduct of your public and punish those who take bribes, I would soon not have a single subject left." But blood was already spilled and, like famished barracuda, the Commons were in full pursuit of Bacon. The great man was wounded, and he would not escape.

In April, Bacon received the full indictment against him, twenty-eight separate charges. It was a sorry bag—a purse from Lady Wharton, a cabinet from Sir John Kennedy, gold buttons from someone else . . . the list droned on. Bacon, now ill as much with a corrosion of his heart as ailment of his body, sank into a helpless torpor. He finally answered the charges without defending himself, writing to Parliament that "I am guilty of corruption, and do renounce all defense, and put myself upon the grace and mercy of your Lordships."

Soon, a scene took place that Bacon must have shrunk from, so degrading must it have been for him. Twelve peers of the realm called on Bacon at York House and regarded him solemnly as he lay in his bed, too sick to stand and talk. Catherine Drinker Bowen reports the scene in which Bacon beseechingly pleaded for mercy. "My lords, it is my act, my hand, my heart. Be merciful to a broken reed." They went away unmoved. In a few days, more peers came, this time to fetch the Great Seal—symbol and visible evidence of the authority of the Lord Chancellor. Again Miss Bowen tells us the lords' response: "We wish it had been better with you."

"The worse, the better," was Bacon's weary, resigned reply. "God gave it, by my own fault I have lost it."

Next, the Lords sat in judgment to determine the punishment. The wheel came full circle, for on the tribunal of the Lords were two of Bacon's mortal enemies: the Earl of Suffolk, who had been tossed out of office for embezzlement (Bacon had been one of his judges); and the Earl of Southampton, who was Essex's partner and who remembered all too bitterly Bacon's defection from his sponsor and friend.

The awful question, to Bacon, was whether he would be sentenced to "degradation," which meant the loss of his titles. By two votes, degradation was avoided. Bacon was condemned to pay a fine of forty thousand pounds and to be imprisoned in the Tower during the King's pleasure. He was declared incapable of holding any office in the state or of sitting in Parliament, and he was banished for life from the verge of the court. "In such misery and shame ended that long career of worldly wisdom and worldly prosperity," was Macaulay's verdict.

Sir Edward Coke, foremost lawyer of his age and Bacon's mightiest enemy, stood in the forefront of the House when the sentence was read. Though there is no historical fact to sustain it, one may imagine that Coke smiled a terrible, satisfied smile. Thus was politically extinguished the largest light of the century.

What was the prompting that caused a man of Bacon's sensitivity and intelligence to become the child of acquisitiveness? Perhaps it was the too-long obscurity, the indifference of the court to his abilities, and the nagging fear that he would again be poor.

Macaulay lacerates Bacon with merciless prose: "How dare Bacon insist," he writes, "that taking gifts was a harmless exercise of the times, and what distortion of logic does the Chancellor deal in when he counts lining his own purse as part of the perquisites of the office? By whatever standard one chooses to apply, the Bacon affair turns squalid."

Public men in the twentieth century can well ponder the fate and misery of Bacon. The demands of public office strain the purse of politicians of modest means. The expense of traveling between Capitol Hill and his home district can bankrupt a congressman without supplementing income. How, then, does a man without independent means manage to fulfill his public duties, be among his constituents frequently, campaign incessantly, feed, clothe, and educate his family, and still live within the salary and perquisites of a congressman or a senator or, for that matter, a mayor or councilman?

When do campaign funds and personal expenses blend, or are they always separate and unmixable? Is the public servant without ample means to wage political war with a rich opponent under ground rules that make one's personal wealth weigh the scales in the rich man's favor? If that be the case, is this patently unfair to the poor man? And if not, what are the regulations for fund-raising opportunities, and how may the contributions be used? Are not everyday living expenses as much a part of the public man's overall expenses as the payment of television time, pamphlets, and organized political effort? Where and how is the line drawn?

The answers are not yet found by this nation. Yet there ought to be certified boundaries in which all citizens may freely compete for public office without the advantage of wealth, inherited or otherwise, or the disadvantage of an empty estate.

A public man ought to have the right to organize an expense fund, independently managed by outside parties, with all contributors registered and publicly known, with contributions limited to a ceiling figure. In this way, a congressman can retrieve travel, staff, and constituent expenses without savage attrition of his own slender pocketbook and borrowing capacity. Moreover, every mayor, congressman, and senator ought to have an expense account, nontaxable, to use for political expenditures connected with his office. And finally, the laws governing contributions ought to be reordered to cut away all the subterfuges and comical exemptions that now exist. The shadowed passing of money from private citizen to public man, so long tolerated, ought to be systematized and made open for anyone to look at.

The rules of the political television game need to be spelled out specifically, and tough sanctions enforced against those who break the rules.

It is a truism of the twentieth century that television is the most cataclysmic force in politics. It is quite possible for an obscure, wealthy man out of office to defeat consistently a renowned, poor man in office by the skilled use of television. The money needed is large, so large that it boggles the mind to consider it. In the six to ten largest states, $1 million or more can be spent usefully on television in a hot primary election, and the same amount and more in the general election campaign.

And the statistics jolt the imagination. More people will watch the network news shows of NBC, ABC, and CBS in two nights than will see all the movies in all the theaters in this country in one month. Each day, approximately 63 million newspapers are delivered or sold in newsstands throughout the nation; but the largest newspaper in the country has a circulation of no more than 2 million daily. Yet, a single network news show will produce 20 to 30 million viewers in a single evening. A ten-second, twenty-second, or one-minute spot announcement for a political candidate will gather an audience in the nation of 30 to 50 million, depending on the show in which it is shown, or on the popularity of the shows it is adjacent to. The impact and intensity of a creatively skilled political message is so spacious that there is no known way to measure it adequately.

The dollar amounts are staggering.

Based on research developed from newspaper reports, magazines, congressional committees, the Federal Communications Commission, and the Citizens Research Foundation in Princeton, New Jersey, some credible figures are uncovered.

It is estimated that approximately $50 million was spent nationally for television and radio time for political advertising during the 1970 elections. This is a 56% increase over the expenditure of $32.1 million for broadcast time in the prior non-Presidential year elections of 1966. (There is some evidence that this dollar estimate and percentage increases are low, and when more definite figures are in, these estimates will go up.)

The estimates include both the primary and the general election. To these time charges must be added production and promotion costs, fees, and commissions to obtain the grand total of political outlays for television and radio time. Such total costs in 1970 are estimated to be in the vicinity of $62 million.

Based on these research sources, here is a chart showing the fast-rising curve of broadcast time and production cost expenditures in the U. S. elections of 1962, 1964, 1966, and 1968:

BROADCAST EXPENDITURES IN PRIOR ELECTIONS
(*In Millions of Dollars*)

General Elections	*1962*	*1964*	*1966*	*1968*
TV Time	7.7	17.5	12.0	27.1
Radio Time	4.5	7.1	7.8	13.3
Primaries				
TV Time	4.9	6.3	7.0	10.9
Radio Time	3.2	3.7	5.3	7.6
Total for Time	20.3	34.6	32.1	58.9
Add Estimated 25% for Production and Promotion Costs, etc.	5.1	8.7	8.0	14.7
Grand Total	25.4	43.3	40.1	73.6

In races for *senator* only in the general election (not including primaries) of 1970, in *four* states, New York, Illinois, California, and Texas, some $4.2 million was spent on broadcast time alone.

On New York City's six major television stations, candidates for governor and senator plus two New Jersey senatorial candidates, spent a grand total of $2.7 million. Note again, this enormous sum of money for just *six* stations in New York City.

That is why today television is such a gargantuan mountain

of a force that no set of rational rules governing sensible campaigning can ignore it.

An election format which a modern nation might consider is one in which all television spot (10-second, 30-second, one-minute) announcements are barred from the screen. They are fiendishly efficient, and even if regulations set the number that could be displayed, the candidate with the brightest, sharpest, and best-paid professional image-makers would still win. And even then if limits were put on production costs, there would always be sly and discreet ways to bounce around the rules. Any brief message that is capable of an impact to persuade a voter to change his mind—and his vote—is a capability that rides hard against fair play in the polling booth. The wealthy candidate can always gather in the best this new legerdemain has to offer, and the breedings of new and even more clever Mesmers would only serve to lift the bidding, not balance the scales.

Second, only personal appearances by the candidate would be allowed on television, and the use of film or other professionally prepared material would be barred. It would be just the candidate talking to the people, without gimmicks or quick cuts or voice-over or soft-focus or edited endorsements. The candidate must be served up unadorned, with nothing save his voice and brain and instincts to guide him and garment him.

Third, free time should be made available in five-minute or fifteen-minute slots to all primary and general election opponents in certain state and federal races. This can be fixed by impartial boards in the states for those campaigns for state offices and by a federal commission for those offices which are federal. (A problem that most people do not consider is the waste of audiences that some candidates must pay for. In New Jersey and Maryland, for example, candidates must pay for time over New York City and Washington, D. C. stations for audiences that cannot vote for them because they are out of the districts in which the campaigns are being waged.)

Therefore, in addition to free time, as specified, discount rates, honest discount rates must apply to all political television time. In other words, the political candidate ought to have the right to purchase over federally franchised television outlets a rate for time that is less than a product being advertised for sale.

Finally, there must be a limit, a tough regulation toughly enforced, on all television expenditures. The limit can be in time or money, but it ought to be clear and it ought to be policed.

Fourth, *all* campaigning costs, for print advertising, direct mail, headquarters, staff, canvassers, and everything must be limited, and audited with such strictness that they can never be exceeded.

It might also be interesting, really interesting, to see what would happen if the public insisted that no candidate ever address an audience, particularly a TV audience, with a prepared address created by some anonymous speechwriter. Today, no one can ever be sure whose words the candidate speaks. His voice ought to be the carrier of his own words, not the purchasable talents of a professional writer, adviser, or agent. Obviously, a candidate cannot personally write every document or declaration he sets forth. But there is sound reason to insist that whenever he speaks to his constituency, what he says should be truly his, coming from what he believes and feels, and expressed in prose that he constructs. At the very least, there ought to be an honest footnoting accompanying the public papers of every governor, congressman, senator, and President which candidly states: "This speech by Senator Grandspeak was written by Melvin Goodwrite." An audience ought to be able, after a particularly fine piece of oratory, to rise and shout: "Author! Author!"

All the above are stern measures. But they can be taken and ought to be taken if there is to remain within the American political arena a parity of opportunity for rich and poor to contest for political leadership.

The people have a right, made more urgent in this age of

glossy communications, to appraise the man, not the packaged product.

The folly of ignoring this terrible crisis of campaigning costs can be a great American tragedy. It is neither fair nor sensible to allow Congress, the State House, or the White House to go to the men with the most money or the richest friends. While we argue and fret about national priorities, there is not enough attention given to the priority which would make it possible for every man in the land to have an equal chance to fill a public office. If we lag in this objective we will be encouraging a formula that would open high political office only to the men who must either have inherited money, or made it, or married it, or who put themselves in the debt (and obligation) of those who are rich—and possibly ambitious.

Finally, the salaries of city and county officials, in too many localities so sadly undervalued, must be raised to levels to which the best men could be attracted without abusing the lives and comfort of their families. It is almost obscenely foolish that a city, say Houston, Texas, the sixth largest in the nation, should pay its mayor $20,000 a year plus a paltry expense account. It is as if the city and its citizens place such little faith in its government that they plainly state: "Only millionaires need apply."

(It is a matter of some tragedy that mayors as a group are rudely treated by the electorate when they aspire to higher office. With the possible exception of Hubert Humphrey, former mayor of Minneapolis, one is hard put to name any mayor of a large American city who has been able to navigate past the political rapids of his own city. Most of the time they are swept up on the shore, battered remnants of political figures who were so scarred by the rip tides of city government that they lie there, bleak reminders of the high price one pays to be a mayor of any large American city today.)

The plight of Francis Bacon in the seventeenth century is relevant to the problems of money in politics in the twentieth century if only to emphasize that the problem is of long endurance, and in the United States the problem is still unsolved.

Bacon's problems came from his large desires, or perhaps what he believed to be the style of living the first public man in the kingdom ought to be entitled to. If he was wrong about the dimensions of those desires, at least he could comment incisively about how the lack of money affects a public servant's conscience—and his conduct.

And probably as he fell the long fall, he might have concluded that all life for him was over, that after his scandal and failure, there was nothing left for him to achieve. But Bacon had five years remaining. Almost from the hour of his downfall and exile, he never stopped working. He commenced a digest of the laws of England, a history of England under the princes of the house of Tudor, a body of natural history, a philosophical romance, and a Latin translation of *The Advancement of Learning,* with seven new parts added, including *The New Atlantis.* His immortal work, *Novum Organum,* published the year before his public demise, was making him one of the towering figures of the world.

He was sad but not defeated. He felt the harsh hiss of public scorn, and it pained him. "No receipt openeth the heart but a true friend," he wrote. "For a crowd is not a company, and faces are but a gallery of pictures, and talk but a tinkling cymbal, when there is no love."

He knew the gall of humiliation. But like politicians, first ministers, and monarchs, he understood that the inner man is revealed when he is pushed to the wall and a thousand daggers press against his stomach. "In the business of life," he wrote, "a man's disposition and the secret workings of his mind and affections are better discovered when he is in trouble than at other times."

There are few men in history who have Bacon's insight into modern matters, though his foresight was curiously lacking in the appraisal of his own conduct. He understood as few men did the interplay of human emotions and the part they play in both conspiracy and achievement. His advice on the avoidance of revolutions is as sound today as when he first uttered it:

> The surest way to prevent seditions . . . is to take away the matter of them; for if there be fuel prepared, it is hard to tell whence the spark shall come that shall set it on fire . . . neither does it follow that the suppressing of discussion with too much severity should be a remedy of troubles . . . the matter of sedition is of two kinds: much poverty and much discontentment. . . . The cue of every leader, of course, is to divide his enemies and to unite his friends. . . . A better recipe for the avoidance of revolutions is an equitable distribution of wealth: Money is like muck, not good unless it be spread.

In his essay "Of Youth and Age," he probably compressed into shorter space more wisdom about the generation gap than anyone before or after.

> Young men are fitter to invent than to judge, fitter for execution than for counsel and fitter for new projects than for settled business . . . young men in the conduct and management of actions, embrace more than they can hold, stir more than they can quiet; fly to the end without consideration of the means and degrees; pursue absurdly some few principles which they have chanced upon. Men of age object too much, consult too long, adventure too little, repent too soon . . . and content themselves with a mediocrity of success.

Then he summed up with graceful neatness the proper form for a generational armistice: "Certainly it is good to compel employment of both [the young and the old] because the virtues of either may correct the defects of both."

To every politician operating actively in the arena today, Bacon had a piece of advice which the old professionals in Washington and in state capitols and city halls around the country know so well to be true. Will Durant summed up Bacon's political philosophy this way:

> In politics as in love, it does not do to give one's self wholly; one should at all times give, but at no time all. Gratitude is nourished with expectation.

Bacon died of pneumonia, brought about by his investigating the possibilities of refrigeration by stuffing a hen with snow. He never expressed a fear of death. One of his last writings was a line that surfaced again three hundred years later in another clime and another time, and was the kindle wood that fired a nation. Said Bacon: "Nothing is to be feared except fear itself."

VOLTAIRE:

TIMELESS EMINENCE

Once there was a superb old courtesan named Ninon de Lenclos, who, in her eighty-fourth year, became attracted to the bright mind of the ten-year-old son of her notary and author of her will, one M. Arouet. Young François-Marie Arouet, she thought, will become a credit to his nation if his mind is employed usefully. She told her notary that she would leave two thousand francs in her will to the young boy if the father would buy him books to read. The famous courtesan died, the books were bought, the boy read them, and grew up to become Voltaire.

If one believes the story, then Ninon's legacy may well have marked the most spectacular outcropping of wit and arrogance and literary splendor of all time.

François-Marie Arouet was born in Paris on November 21, 1694. His mother was Marie Marguerite d'Aumard, of fragmentary noble lineage. He was the youngest of five children, so puny and sickly at birth that no one gave him long to live. Throughout his life, he suffered illness, real, imaginary, and contrived; never, to hear him tell it, did he manage a day without some intrusion of ill health. He lived to be eighty-four.

Voltaire is a timeless eminence. He mingled in his person and in his creativity immense wit and wittiness, a very solid pragmatism, and a very inflammable idealism. He possessed bottomless energy: he had a business acumen that made him, and kept him, a millionaire with shrewd investments before which any Wall Street house would genuflect in appreciative awe; he was educated by Jesuits and scoffed at some of the rites of organized religion.

He hated laziness, never understood the idle mind or person, and never allowed himself not to work; he left an enormous bulk of writing—more than fifty plays, countless poems (a bare catalogue of them fills fourteen royal octavo columns), numberless tales (of which *Candide* is the most perfected), histories, general criticism and miscellaneous writing, and correspondence (tons of it) to most of the eminent literary lights, rising and fading kinglets, princes of the blood, and mistresses (his and others) in Europe. Voltaire was the sauciest, angriest, the most prolific, and, possibly, when it served him practically to be so, the most mendacious of all letter writers.

There was nothing odd about Voltaire; he liked women, loved most of them, was capable of faithfulness and faithlessness and could plausibly justify either. With a matchless aplomb he was kind to husbands of the wives he made love to, even managing to live for fourteen years with Madame du Châtelet *and* her husband, who had the good sense to spend most of his time with his regiment. (It is an indicator of French tolerant morals that society was less surprised at the marquess's acquiescence than the lovers' fidelity.) One of Voltaire's early tutors was the Abbé de Chaulieu, who declared, with solemn finality, that wine and women were the most delectable boons granted to man by a wise and beneficent Nature. Voltaire did not need urging to take up this regimen. However delightful the pleasures of the flesh, though, they never diverted him from the compulsion to work.

Voltaire had a horror of being ponderous or heavy-footed. He suffered bores, boredom, and pundits with ill grace, viewing them with the same distaste he democratically felt for some reigning monarchs and rival literary lions. He resented the "profusion of useless things with which they wished to load my brain. My motto is, *to the point.*" His whole life consisted of work, fleeing into exile, returning, and then fleeing again, journeying from one mistress to another, from one temporary home to another, and finally returning to die in Paris after an exile of twenty-eight years.

Posterity honors him; and women, and society in general, found him irresistible (though it must be explained that living with Voltaire over a long stretch of time was, to many of his hosts and hostesses, like living with a gorgeous lion who, in fretful moments, gulped down a head or two). It must have been Voltaire who first lived the old show-biz tenet, "Always leave them laughing." There is little doubt from the historical record of the time that he was the funniest man alive. No other reason would explain his immunity from a constant caning and ostracism, so freely did he attack the mightiest, the highest-born, and the church.

Will Durant describes how in 1742 in Paris Voltaire was coaching Mlle Dumesnil in a difficult scene in Voltaire's play *Mérope*. She gasped that she would have to have "the very devil" in her to properly and passionately play the scene. "Ah," said Voltaire, "that is just it, for you must have the devil in you to succeed in any of the arts." No one, wrote Durant, better fitted that requirement than Voltaire. De Maistre called him the man "into whose hands hell had given all its powers."

It is possible that Voltaire would smilingly agree. He was not in continual conflict with the devil, and hell to him was only a geographical and temporary area where depressed spirits visited from time to time, and to which Voltaire would on occasion consign his enemies.

Moreover, he was truly what Catherine of Russia had called him: "the divinity of gaiety." Said Voltaire, in confirmation of Catherine's description: "If Nature had not made us a little frivolous, we should be most wretched. It is because one can be frivolous that the majority do not hang themselves." Voltaire added: "Woe to philosophers who cannot laugh away their wrinkles. I look upon solemnity as a disease."

He had no respect for systems and the rubric of certainty. It was his judgment that "every chief of a sect in philosophy has been a little of a quack. The further I go, the more I am confirmed in the idea that systems of metaphysics are for philosophers what novels are for women. It is only charlatans who are certain."

While he lived in England for some three years as a young man he met Congreve, and gushingly advised the great playwright that he regarded him as a peer of Molière. Congreve replied, "Ah, but I had rather you wished to meet me because I am an English gentleman." To which Voltaire sniffed: "There are too many English gentlemen, and too few great playwrights."

He had a facile genius for enlivening the ideas of others, though he demolished egos and poured salt into hidden wounds. "If I had not cheered up the subject nobody would have been scandalized, but then nobody would have read me," is Voltaire's credo, anticipating Hilaire Belloc's ". . . when I am dead, I hope it may be said: 'His sins were scarlet, but his books were read.' "

He was a great moneylender, from whence came a good part of his income. He lent money to an Abbé MacCarthy, who had gone to the East without repaying him. Voltaire learned that the Abbé, in Constantinople, had been circumcised and impaled. "Ah," murmured Voltaire, "many people have owed me money, but so far none of them have been impaled."

Voltaire detested critics, an attitude not so uncommon in modern America. He called them "insects of a single day." Voltaire gave short shrift to the intellectuals of the time who declaimed about the greatness of art and writing which an unappreciative public was too dumb to recognize. He fervently believed that a play which does not succeed in the theater is a bad play, and a book allowed to go out of print a poor book. "No interesting play ever fails," he said. It was his avowal that there was a sufficient number of educated playgoers in Paris, and he was prepared to accept their judgment. Voltaire may have been tempted to this belief by the fact that all his books were runaway best sellers and nearly all his plays were embraced joyously by the public.

Voltaire was remarkably free of temperament when he was working. He was an easy collaborator. He would shorten, lengthen, or alter verses, and even be cooperative about words he used. It was his belief that a fresh eye often perceives small inadequacies that the author by himself might never notice. It is proper to muse about Voltaire's mixing today with some screen writers, playwrights, novelists, many of whom have a fixed view that every word they write has surely been transported from the summit of Mount Sinai, suitably engraved on tablets of stone.

Not unsurprisingly, Voltaire thought that his plays did have a measure of immortality and were capable of inspiring a suitable passion in those who acted in them. Once he heard about a rich old Londoner named Bond, who produced Voltaire's play *Zaïre* and took the role of Zaïre's father. On the night the play opened, the elderly gentleman threw himself into the part with such fervor that when the moment came for him to expire in Zaïre's arms he did, actually, die. Voltaire heartily approved.

Voltaire hated splendidly. One for whom he had an unspeakable distaste was the poet Jean-Baptiste Rousseau. He remarked once about Rousseau's *Ode to Posterity:* "I really do not believe this ode will ever reach its address." He got a perverse joy out of flailing the hides of the hangers-on at court. When the Regent, the duc d'Orléans, felt the need to economize and began by cutting in half the number of horses in the royal stables, Voltaire quipped "He could have done better to dismiss half the asses that crowded his Majesty's court."

Like so many mortals, Voltaire examined his own conscience and found it in good shape, whereas he was not so obliging about the motives of others. He professed pacifism. Warring princes were to him "hateful spiders tearing each other to pieces instead of spinning silk." He harangued Frederick the Great by admonishing him to quit ravaging the earth. Frederick knew his man. "It's the fashion now to make war," said the King, "and presumably it will last a good long while. But I can remember the time when if you had an army, you would have marched against Desfontaines, Rousseau, and Van Duren" (three of Voltaire's mortal enemies). Voltaire's answer is not recorded.

Though Voltaire engaged in an on-again, off-again friendship and dialogue with Frederick, he was not above banging the monarch on the jowls. Frederick won a great victory at Mollwitz, but the story has it that when the battle was going badly Frederick spurred his horse wildly to the rear and only returned later when the battle had been won. Voltaire's comment was that the only living creature to whom Frederick ever felt gratitude was the horse that bore him from Mollwitz.

When he wanted something desperately, he didn't hesitate to go right to the top. Once, staying in the duchy of Lorraine, which was presided over by the Queen's father, Stanislas, the King of Poland, Voltaire began his letter of importuning: "Sire, when one is in Paradise it is to God that one must address oneself." In this case, Voltaire was thwarted by Stanislas's treasurer, who rapped the Voltairean knuckles and, in so many words, told him he was a boor.

Voltaire was a genius at many things, and getting into scrapes, alas, was one of them. There were those in France who were certain that Voltaire would get into trouble even in a Trappist monastery. But no one could accuse him of not rising to challenge when the occasion demanded. His insouciance was never more strained than the evening when he surprised Mme du Châtelet and a guardsman named Saint-Lambert in what may be described as a compromising moment. Voltaire was obviously, at first, furious. Emilie assured him of her eternal love, and then Saint-Lambert apologized, and that evening the three supped together. Voltaire told Saint-Lambert: "You are in a happy age of love and delight. Enjoy these moments, too brief. An old invalid like me is not made for these pleasures." He was fifty-four.

Voltaire was, beyond question, the leader in infusing the Newtonian idea into the French intellectual bloodstream. He spread through France a concern for how things work and not with their "essence." Along with Maupertuis and d'Alembert, he changed in a substantial way the direction of French thought, pointing it toward the "practical." Reform in France began with Voltaire. And though the mobs, still milling in an invisible discontent, did not know it, their future power was given a solid philosophical footing.

Voltaire was no democrat in the twentieth-century sense. But in despising cant, laughing at tribal rites, and crying out against abuses of law, justice, and natural reason, he was clearly in the democratic tradition and an early architect of current college dissent. In France, still squirming under the rule if not the person of Louis XIV, Voltaire and the bite of his comic satire were explosively revolutionary.

He broke the link between the brutal *condottiere* and the intellectual. "I do not like heroes," said Voltaire. "They make too much noise in the world." He opened a chasm, since grown steadily larger, between the intellectual and the prince, between the man of thought and the man of action.

Voltaire worked, though, in the milieu of the moment, which demanded to know, if the world is to be reformed, who would lead the reconstruction. Voltaire, like Erasmus and Luther, placed his faith in the enlightened despot. This was not the answer, but without this opening, the road to the future would have been more difficult for democracy to travel. Moreover, it was Voltaire who took pride in and gave praise for Locke and his then curious ideas about government and the consent of the governed. It may be possible to say that had there been no Voltaire stirring the air with new thought—the mingling of English empiricism and the French method of doubt—the Revolution might have been longer in coming.

In his late seventies, in 1771, Voltaire, throwing aside the pessimism of old age, trumpeted a note of hope: "Well-constituted minds are now very numerous; they are at the head of nations; they influence public manners, and year by year the fanaticism that overspread the earth is receding. Stupidity is being at every instant undermined by reason, which is establishing its reign."

That may have been one of the old man's few bad prophecies. He underrated the staying power of fanatics and stupidity. Moreover, there is no mortal to whom what Pascal called "the glory, the jest and riddle of the world" unveiled itself totally, not even to Voltaire. But Voltaire perhaps came as close as anyone, and he did it with a comic thrust, a savoring wisdom, and a deflating irony.

However, Voltaire was always running, always in exile. For him there was no homeland. France, from whose bosom he sprang, never allowed its hospitality to linger, always official France rejected him, and though Voltaire would not have liked the public to glimpse him off stage, with no dissembling, he would have had to admit that with all his wealth and fame and the fear that others felt about his pen, he was lonely. The Emersonian maxim that for every loss there is a gain, and for every gain there is a loss applied with as much efficacy to Voltaire as to anyone, and the old Philosopher would have confessed it so.

One of Voltaire's numerous antagonists was an idle nobleman, the chevalier de Rohan-Chabot. When Voltaire was thirty, the chevalier set a band of ruffians on him. The hooligans were about to beat him into insensibility when the chevalier, directing the activity from the sanctity and safety of his carriage, cried out: "Don't strike his head, something good may come out of that."

This may be recorded as the century's most accurate prophecy.

John Randolph of Roanoke:

THE LAST IDEALIST

It is a matter of more than coincidence that John Randolph of Roanoke lived his early life on a family estate in Virginia named "Bizarre."

Never have residence and temperament been more congenially joined, for in truth Randolph must be accounted as one of the strangest, most unstable men involved in the public life of the nation. He was the precursor of both radical and conservative thought in America—a sticky contradiction that would tax the capability of almost any other man except Randolph. While Students for a Democratic Society might deny it, as one might turn the picture of an errant relative to the wall, Randolph is their spiritual godfather, even as his blood strain runs in the veins of the Liberty Lobby.

For a third of a century he served the country; first as congressman, as Thomas Jefferson's floor leader in the House of Representatives, as senator from Virginia, as United States ambassador to Russia, and as delegate to the Constitutional Convention in Virginia. But Gerald Johnson, in his study of Randolph, insists that what history remembers of this odd nonconformist is "for carrying the wickedest tongue that ever hung in the head of an American congressman, who had the courage and the wit to use it."

The anthologies remember Randolph. They are fat with examples of his parliamentary epigrams. Randolph is the most quotable of a large gallery of quotable American politicians.

In his childhood, he fed ravenously on books. Before he was eleven, he had read Voltaire's *Charles XII,* the *Spectator, Humphry Clinker, The Arabian Nights,* the plays of Shakespeare, *Don Quixote,* Plutarch, Pope's *Homer, Robinson Crusoe, Gulliver's Travels, Orlando Furioso,* Thomson's *Seasons,* and Goldsmith's two-volume *Roman History*. He mentions all this in a letter to a friend, and goes on to say "if from my life were to be taken the pleasure derived from that faculty [of reading] very little would remain. Shakespeare, Milton, Chaucer, Spenser . . . have made up more than half of my worldly enjoyment. To these ought to be added Ovid, Ariosto, Dryden, Beaumont and Fletcher, Otway, Congreve, Sheridan, Addison, Young, Gay, Gray, Cowper, Byron, Aesop, La Fontaine, Rousseau, but above all Burke."

This immense scholarship was to pay dividends later, for he drew from his reading all the source material that was to furnish his speeches with the aptness of phrase that sent so many enemies flying helter-skelter in disarray and fear.

This reading then was his arsenal, and from it he fashioned his own personal armament.

The Randolph weaponry was all encased in a tutored wit, compact, savage, luxuriant, malignant. He attacked, singly and together, the most formidable men in the Republic, and not one escaped his thrusts without breathing a sigh of relief, the kind Theseus surely felt when finally he was rid of the Minotaur. Jefferson, Madison, John Marshall, Calhoun, John Quincy Adams, Clay, Webster, Andrew Jackson, all were terrorized by Randolph's prose lash.

It is impossible to begin an understanding of Randolph unless one knows something about his early life, for what occurred when he was young beckons to all the torment and talent that engulfed him later.

He often referred to "my unprosperous life, the fruit of an ungovernable temper." His father had much to do with it, for he was a vengeful man, and perhaps this strand of poison threaded its way somehow into Randolph. He was miserable in school, hated formal schooling, hated his schoolmaster, hated him with such intensity that he later described the teacher as "the most peevish and ill-tempered of all pedagogues."

There ought to have been some hint of the instability in him when in his first year in Princeton he accused one of his instructors, an eminent professor, of embezzling his funds. That the charge was false did not stop him from repeating it against another teacher in another school! If his mother had lived, she might have laid a restraining hand on the uncontained temper which in outlook and direction each day grew more undisciplined. But she died too early, before the restraint could take root.

Then there occurred an event, even today darkly lit, shadowed by a remote, untenable proof, which might have explained even more. The only record of it is a line in a letter Randolph wrote to his nephew twenty years later: ". . . on my way to Williamsburg, I was taken with scarlet fever and brought to the brink of the grave; so few charms had life for me, so strong was the disgust that I had taken to the world that I was indifferent to the issue of my disease."

Randolph was impotent throughout his life, and this may have been the cause. It is clear that from this day forward his emotions were disfigured. Of the fact that Randolph was scarred by some malediction of fate or heredity or illness, there is little doubt. He remained all his life a beardless, high-voiced figure, with the lank, lean physique of an Ichabod Crane. From a distance he gave the appearance of a young boy.

Once when Randolph was at the height of his powers, a visitor to the gallery of the House of Representatives inquired who was the youth now in the midst of a stirring harangue to the members.

"Why sir," a friend responded, "that is the great Mr. Randolph of Virginia."

The visitor's jaw hung slack at his incredible reply, for in truth the speaker in the chamber of the House had the form and profile of a lad in his twenties, not an aging man nearing fifty. There was an unjust mockery in this deception so sorely worn by Randolph, and so opposed to the reality that became visible on closer inspection: the latticed wrinkles, intersecting lines of self-reproach laced over skin that resembled crepe; the gaunt, pinched shoulders atop a frail, long, thin frame.

John Quincy Adams cast about for the most venomous brevity available to describe adequately the despicable man, for whom Adams had a remorseless distaste. Adams reached back to Ovid to pluck out a verse that gave Randolph his just due, as Adams saw that due:

> His face is ashen; meagre his whole body,
> His breast is green with gall;
> Suffused with poison his tongue.

There were many who would endorse the Adams damning, and who would account the resemblance perfect; even as there were still others who would suggest the lines fit Adams as well as they measured Randolph. Both the sixth president and the Virginia congressman had the ability to lift hatred to a gorgeous level of artistry.

(Henry Adams, grandson of John Quincy Adams, in his biography of Randolph, which, as one might suppose, is something less than grandly favorable to the Virginian, suggests that his grandfather might have chosen another of Ovid's verses to describe Randolph more sharply:

> He sees with pain men's good fortune,
> And pines in seeing; he taunts and is mocked at once;
> And is his own torture.

No matter how bitchily applied by Henry Adams, there is aptness in these Ovid lines.)

Randolph was, unaccountably and consistently, the American radical who became the archetypical conservative, and gave color and light to all the conservatives who followed him. He is important in American political history not so much for his literary and oratorical style, though they were of a measure considerable and spacious enough to influence succeeding generations, but mainly because the conservative ideas and formulas to which he gave form and vigor flowered for years after his death; and indeed today one can hear his echoes in various parts of the political arena.

He was passionate in what he believed and denounced.

His great asset was his great fault. He never bent. He never turned or changed. From 1803 to 1833, his course was a straight line, his consistency perfect, an inflexibility that, if anything, grew more rigid as he grew older.

He was the first advocate of civil rights, though its meaning to him would not be shared by twentieth-century members of the American Civil Liberties Union. He despised a federal authority that threatened the freedom of any man. His sense of personal freedom was so strong that it defied every piece of legislation which enlarged in any way the federal embrace. His personal creed was his famous aphorism: "I am an aristocrat. I love liberty. I hate equality." By this he meant he detested any law that stunted one man as it sought to lengthen another.

He emphasized the principle that a legislator should stay close to the people he represented. The idea that lawmakers act for the people as a whole repulsed him. His particular constituency was his first concern. They sent him to Congress, and by damn, he would represent them. Thus local rights—the rights not of the nation but of the community—called for his attention.

(Randolph was a soul brother to Bernadette Devlin, the fiery, twenty-three-year-old member of Parliament from Ulster. On "Meet the Press," August 24, 1969, when asked by a questioner why she was not in the streets trying to make peace instead of manning the barricades with her fire-bombing, rock-throwing constituents, Miss Devlin answered: "I was where I belonged. I was sent to Parliament by 68,000 people of Northern Ireland and

I represent them and no one else." One can hear Randolph shouting a joyous "Bravo, Bernadette!")

There is a strange familiarity in Randolph's view of justice that sits snugly within the view of the New Left today. He believed that men should obey a constitution only so long as it did not fall in partisan hands—i.e., hands hostile to Randolph and his followers. The basis of authority rested, according to Randolph, on the citizen's view of justice, not the constitution's view of justice. Unjust laws, he thought, should not be obeyed, if the unjust law collided with a stable belief of the citizen. When this conflict occurred, the citizen had the right to defend his liberties by any means. The young latter-day radical who demands the authority to be personal witness to unjust laws and to defy them would be a Randolph man.

Listen to Randolph on his philosophy, as he spoke on a bill which he considered outrageous:

> I consider the Constitution a dead letter. You may entrench yourself in parchment as Lord Chatham said, but the sword will find its way to the vitals of the Constitution. I have no faith in parchment, sir, I have no faith in the abracadabra of the Constitution. If under a power to regulate trade you draw the last drop of blood from our veins, what are the checks of the Constitution to us? A fig for the Constitution! When the scorpion's sting is probing us to the quick, shall we pause to chop logic? Shall we let some learned and cunning clerk to say whether the power to do this is to be found in the Constitution and then if he, from whatever motive, shall maintain the affirmative, like the animal whose fleece forms so material a part of this bill, quietly lie down and be sheared.

No matter how you slice it, this is a call to destroy "the system." No wonder the manifesto of the young revolutionaries sounds so familiar.

Randolph's source of philosophical instruction is Edmund Burke. Randolph (and Burke) define the real rights of man upon the classic rostrum of justice: to each his own. Men have a right to the benefits of civil society, to do justice, to have the fruits of their industry, to instruction in life and to consolation in death, but no rights to equality at the expense of others, no rights to political power regardless of ability or integrity. Man's rights, as Russell Kirk saw them in his overview of Randolph and his ideas, are not mysterious gifts deduced from *a priori* postulates; they are the opportunities which the stability of a just society bestows on its members. What Randolph believed was that wanting prerogatives was not the same as possessing a right to them.

Thus did Randolph and Jefferson collide in a long and bitter philosophical struggle—the latter an advocate of the Locke school of natural law, and Randolph plumping hard for rights conferred by a civil society.

Randolph was suspicious of majorities. Like modern radicals, he took a jaundiced view of the superior wisdom of the majority. He railed against rigid qualifications for merit, for example. When Virginia set a minimum of thirty years of age for election to the House of Delegates, he raged. It was all right, he said, that the state might conclude that few young men acquire political influence, but it was unwise and unjust to shut out all young men by age requirements, regardless of merit.

He had no fondness for the larger group setting tax rates, for another example. "King Numbers" he called the system of the majority making rules for taxation. He fumed: "I will put it in the power of no man or set of men who ever lived to tax me without my consent. . . ."

When he turned on Jefferson, the Sage of Monticello never endured a heavier pounding. Randolph cleaved at Jefferson's reach for new ideas, and with comic thrust, ran the butcher's heavy edge down and through Jefferson's public face:

> Sir, if there be any point in which the authority of Mr. Jefferson might be considered valid it is in the mechanism of a plow. For Mr. Jefferson had designed and sent to the savants at Paris

> a model plow, exhibited in the Jardin des Plantes. It was mightily admired by the savants but when applied to the red Virginia clay, in competition with the ill-looking Carey plow, it was beaten as thoroughly as common sense will always beat theory and reveries.

Randolph, said Russell Kirk, found the source of authority not in a mystic nature but fundamentally in force, force tempered by the experience of man and softened by the wise conventions of society. With Aristotle, Randolph believed that man out of society must be either beast or God; there had never been a condition of truly human existence which was not a state of society.

Nothing could have pleased Randolph more than to know, in the last years of Jefferson, that the old ex-President became somewhat frightened by what he considered to be too rapid an intrusion by the federal government into normal rights of the states. Jefferson wrote a friend: "unless action were taken now, we are undone how to check these unconstitutional measures."

Randolph must have chortled, or whatever Randolph did that passed for a chortle. Vindication is such a sweet passion.

However, it was "the wickedest tongue that ever hung in the head of an American congressman" that fascinates most students of the Randolph legend.

When Richard Rush was selected as secretary of the treasury by President John Quincy Adams, Randolph sneered: "Never were abilities so much below mediocrity so well rewarded; no, not when Caligula's horse was made Consul."

Edward Livingston, a rather decent fellow, congressman, senator, and secretary of state under Andrew Jackson, fell within Randolph's target aim. Sniffed Randolph about Livingston: "He is a man of splendid abilities, but utterly corrupt. Like rotten mackerel by moonlight, he shines and stinks." Poor Livingston never escaped the canopy of Randolph's brutal remark.

Not for idle frivolity did Randolph add to his family motto the Latin maxim: *Fari quae sentiat*—"say what you think." Probably no family motto was ever lived more truthfully.

He was no modest, blushing violet. When he took his seat for the first time in the House, he was not yet twenty-seven. When the clerk of the House, a bit amazed at the callow youth standing before him, asked him if he were really old enough to be counted present, Randolph pierced him with a cold stare and answered: "Ask my constituents."

The elder Adams, the first John, learned a lesson which high-stationed officials to this hour seemed not to have absorbed: that it is better to ignore the barks and snaps at your heels than to answer and make famous the obscure barker-snapper. Randolph, who thought Adams quite a pompous old fool, wrote the President a letter in which he left out all the flowered salutations that the President felt the office warranted. It was a rather rude piece of prose for a rookie congressman, and Adams called his cabinet into session to receive their views on how to handle this arrogant young intruder. With the full solemn weight of his councilors in hand, the President sent a special message to the Congress chiding certain "matters and style." In essence, the President was asking the Congress to chastise the new member from Virginia. A stumbling idiot could have foretold the result. The House rose as one man to defend their colleague, the President was curtly put down, and Randolph was instantly famous.

He never let the light of eminence die.

When Thomas Jefferson came to power, although Randolph was for a time his floor leader, he found it unsuitable to nourish fidelity to any man for long, or for that matter even the House itself. To the House of Representatives he lashed out with "like all political quacks, you deal only in handbills and nostrums," and for Jefferson's administration he provided a label: "the refuse of the retail trade of politics."

About General James Wilkinson, the highest ranking officer in the Army, he offered this opinion: "Perhaps you never saw human nature in so degraded a situation as in the person of Wilkinson." In fact, his view of Wilkinson was so barren of any value, he filed a bill, in 1810, to abolish the entire military and naval establishments, which puts him one hundred and sixty years in the van of the New Leftists.

For the men in possession of the largest political power, regardless of party, he had only contempt. "There is a fatality, sir, attending plenitude of power," he said, "soon or late some mania seizes upon its possessors; they fall from the dizzy height, through the giddiness of their own heads."

He had little use for the rhetoric of either the office holder or the office seeker. "Man shall not live by bread alone, but mostly by catch phrases," was the way he filed his dissent.

As one who had a horror of an overpowering federal apparatus, and even of the growing grasp of state legislatures, Randolph, in a constitutional convention in Virginia, rose to say:

> The principles of free government in this country . . . have more to fear from overlegislation than from any other cause. Yes, Sir—they have more to fear from armies of legislators and armies of judges than from any other, or from all other causes. Besides the great manufactory at Washington we have twenty-four other laboratories more at work all making laws. . . . Among all these lawyers, judges and legislators, there is a great oppression on the people who are neither lawyers, judges nor legislators. . . . Sir, I can never forget that, in the great and good book, to which I look for all truth and all wisdom, the book of Kings succeeds the book of Judges.

If this is a modern refrain, one would have to admit it is, these days, not being said as elegantly and malignantly as Randolph phrased it.

Once Tristram Burges of Rhode Island rose in the House, a foolhardy volunteer as it turned out, to put Randolph in his place, and proceeded to lacerate the Virginian as best he could. When he finished, Randolph spoke briefly: "You pride yourself, Sir, upon an animal faculty, in respect to which the slave is your equal and the jackass infinitely your superior." Mr. Burges never took on Randolph again.

Another brave but inadequate lancer who rose to joust with Randolph was a congressman from Ohio, one Philomen Beecher by name. Randolph tolerated him for a time, particularly when Beecher would interrupt Randolph by shouting, "Previous question, Mr. Speaker." When this had happened numerous times, Beecher bellowing "Previous question, Mr. Speaker," Randolph turned a baleful glance on the noisy member, and said: "Mr. Speaker, in the Netherlands, a man of small capacity, with bits of wood and leather, will, in a few moments, construct a toy that, with the pressure of the finger and thumb, will cry 'Cuckoo! Cuckoo!' With less ingenuity, and with inferior materials, the people of Ohio have made a toy that will, without much pressure, cry 'Previous Question, Mr. Speaker!'" Amid gales of congressional laughter, Philomen Beecher slunk out of the chamber, and there is no record of his ever tangling with Randolph again.

To a debate whose cause was an appropriations bill to spend more money, Randolph spoke for economy, and ended his remarks with: "That most delicious of all privileges . . . spending other people's money."

Randolph, like most long-distance speakers, could not abide this proclivity in others. When Senator Thomas Hart Benton filibustered for four days, Randolph dryly commented that Benton's speech consumed one day more than the French Revolution of 1830.

It is a marked habit in most men that they view morosely in others that which they ignore in themselves. Randolph once remarked about "the glorious privilege of finding fault, one very dear to the depraved condition of human nature."

The melding of brain and tongue was so swift that no one could be certain of the retort, though all knew it would be forthcoming. He pelted two members of the House when he said about Robert Wright and John Rea (pronounced Ray) that the House of Representatives contained two curious juxapositions: "A Wright always wrong, and a Rea without light."

Once he bore in on a hapless colleague with the statement:

"His mind is like a parcel of land, poor to begin with and rendered more barren by too intensive cultivation."

(To prove that a tart and stylishly constructed line is available for reproduction, some long years later, in 1919, Senator Thaddeus Caraway of Arkansas rose to smite Senator Henry Cabot Lodge of Massachusetts with this piece of spontaneous wit: "I have long heard of the reputation for wisdom and wit of the Senator from Massachusetts, but his speech today has convinced me that his mind is like the land of his native state, barren by nature and impoverished by cultivation." Ah, to possess the skill of the quick retort!)

It may be difficult for the interested observer to understand how Randolph was able to manufacture all his famous sallies, since he was in need of so many of them, so vast was the army of those whom he either distrusted or despised. John Calhoun was one of those in that large array of those he hated, though it is a perversion of logic for Randolph, since it was Calhoun, after Randolph's absence from the scene, who held aloft the banner of Randolph's creed and philosophy and gave gristle and force to Randolph's conservative thought.

Randolph considered Calhoun a man mad with a lust for war, and he never forgave or forgot Calhoun's stand as one of the war hawks who pushed and shoved until the United States was involved in the War of 1812, which Randolph opposed with all the fervor he could summon, which was quite a lot.

When Calhoun was vice president under John Quincy Adams, Randolph once began a speech in the Senate with these words: "Mr. Speaker, I mean Mr. President of the Senate and would-be President of the United States, which God in His infinite mercy avert."

One time a new member came to the House, elected to fill a vacancy of the seat of a man, Randolph's friend, who had died suddenly. The new member almost immediately began to slash away at Randolph, and, to the surprise of the House, Randolph appeared to take no notice, until one afternoon, in discussing a bill in which the dead congressman had a keen interest, Randolph gravely said: ". . . this bill has lost much in the death of my dear friend, whose seat, alas, remains vacant."

One famous story which has the cast of characters ever changing (some say it was Clay involved, others say it was someone else) concerns Randolph meeting Clay on a narrow walking path. Clay said: "I, sir, never step aside for a scoundrel!" (some say the word was not "scoundrel" but "puppy") whereupon Randolph quickly stepped into the mud-filled street, and said: "But on the other hand, I always do. Please pass."

The gift of a concise thrust is one uncommonly known and preciously valued. Randolph had it. He described Martin Van Buren as one "who habitually rowed to his object with muffled oars."

Once he said: "Asking one of the States to surrender part of her sovereignty is like asking a lady to surrender part of her chastity."

How blessed is the reply with a lethal brevity. When a friend told Randolph that a certain congressman was denouncing him, Randolph looked puzzled. "Denounce me? That's strange. I never did him a favor."

When the Congress met again in 1827, John Quincy Adams was president and Henry Clay was secretary of state, and since both of them ranked very high on Randolph's hate list, the aging Virginian brooded sourly, determined to destroy both of them. "I bore some humble part," he growled, "in putting down the dynasty of John the First and by the grace of God I hope to aid in putting down the dynasty of John the Second."

It was just a year before these words, in 1826, that Randolph's most famous attack was made, an assault that nearly cost him his life. Adams's election was still odiously reviewed and remembered by much of the nation, particularly by the Jackson men, who called the entire election a gigantic fraud in which Clay sealed his invidious bargain with Adams, supporting him in the 1824 voting squeaker that had to go to the House of Representatives for final resolution. There in the House, Clay chose Adams over Jackson and was rewarded with the State Department. They were an odd pair, Adams and Clay, the former ascetic, austere, aloof, and very correct; and Clay, a hard-driving man, who was frequently drunk and often gambled, an explosive and, said his enemies, a sinful man. It was a strange turn of fate that constructed these political alignments, for Clay opposed the one man, Jackson, who was his ideological comrade, and Randolph supported Jackson, the man who was to later smite and shatter all that Randolph believed in.

Randolph seized the opportunity to speak on a minor bill in the Congress, of no consequence to history, to hurl a poisonous bolt at Clay and Adams. (For clarity, one must be familiar with the novel *Tom Jones,* by Henry Fielding, which was well known to the educated of the Congress and which included two characters, Black George, a racy, candid scoundrel with some redeeming features, and Blifil, a hypocritical creature.)

Randolph wound up his speech with these words: "I was defeated horse, foot and dragoons, cut up and clean broke down by the coalition of Blifil and Black George—by the combination, unheard of till then, of the Puritan with the blackleg."

The roof blew off on this one. Clay, livid with rage, challenged Randolph to a duel. In the late afternoon of April 18, 1826, these two adversaries met on the Virginia side of the Potomac. One of Randolph's seconds was James Hamilton, later governor of South Carolina at the height of the Nullification struggle with President Jackson. Senator Thomas Hart Benton was a spectator.

Randolph was wearing a thick glove, though his pistol trigger had been filed down so that it would fire with just a touch. As he held it, the barrel pointing to the ground, it went off before the word to fire was given. Clay, graciously, to the horror of his seconds, allowed Randolph to reload. Randolph, apparently, when the signal was given, aimed at Clay's leg, and missed, while Clay's bullet zipped by Randolph's waist. Although Benton tried to stop the duel then, Randolph would have none of it. He insisted that the fight go forward.

The pistols were reloaded. This time Clay's ball passed through Randolph's coat, missing his body. Then Randolph, in a gesture so typically admired by him, raised his pistol above Clay's head and deliberately fired into the sky. The Secretary of State, amazed and possibly grateful, strode forward to grasp Randolph's hand. "You owe me a coat, Mr. Clay," was Randolph's remark.

Although Randolph could not furnish any personal example of an enduring loyalty to any man for a stretch of time, he could at least display a continuous bitterness that toward Jefferson never subsided, but always burned, a steady, heated, envenomed hatred. This distaste may have been fueled because Randolph could never forget that he had once been an acolyte of Jefferson, mesmerized by him at an early age, and his floor captain in the House, as much a part of the building of the Jefferson ethos and apparatus as any man, and a prime craftsman in the organizing of Jefferson's party machinery.

When Randolph was near death, and almost dissolved by the crumbling of what he had vainly cherished and for which he had given his adult life, he perceived that Jefferson, though dead for some six years, still exerted on the nation a splendid prestige soaring so far above any petty influence of his own that the mere thought of it soured and trembled him.

One of his last memorable comments was this satirical diatribe against Jefferson:

> I cannot live in this miserable, undone country, where, as the Turks follow their sacred standard, which is a pair of Mahomet's green breeches, we are governed by the old red breeches of that prince of projectors, St. Thomas of Cantingbury; and surely, Becket himself never had more pilgrims at his shrine than the saint of Monticello.

He was dead a year later, in 1833.

The essential void in Randolph probably can be summed up in the fact that he was an erratic romantic. Indeed it could be argued that he had no place in organized politics because he had no ties to anyone, any party, any ideology except his own and his constituency's. His attitude was truly unreal. He lived in an unreal world, in which what he deemed to be true he expected to be true in fact. As any practicing politician knows by instinct, as Jefferson surely knew, the realities of public policy deal with the world as it is now, not as logic and expectation and idealism determine it to be.

Jefferson had committed an almost fatal blunder by agreeing to Randolph as his floor leader in the House, because Randolph had no sense of loyalty to man or administration, only a fidelity to his own view of right and wrong.

There was the so-called Yazoo scandal in Mississippi, when the Georgia legislature in 1795 sold to speculators most of the land now making up the state of Mississippi, then a part of Georgia's western claims. The following year a new legislature rescinded the sale of the land, and in 1802 Georgia ceded the land to the United States government.

Before the Georgia legislature had acted (when the odor of the deal stank so horribly), the speculators had sold a good deal of the land to innocent people. After the ceding of the land to the government, some so-called "innocent" purchasers banded together and laid a claim on the federal government. A very high-level commission (consisting of Madison, Albert Gallatin, and Levi Lincoln, United States attorney general) decided that while the claims were not exactly clear and in many cases downright unfounded, it was better to pay something than to fight a long drawn-out lawsuit. The decision was made to give the claimants about 9 percent of the total demanded.

When this was revealed to Randolph, he literally exploded with anger. He had been to Georgia and personally investigated the entire Yazoo affair. He was witness to the cynical steal (for in truth this is what Randolph judged it to be) in all its brutal contempt for law and fair play. Even 9 percent was too much for Randolph. "This is bribery," he raged.

It may have been that Randolph assumed that when the blatant larceny was sufficiently unveiled all the government would rally to his side, and with him, demand to kick the rascals in their backside. To his amazement, nothing of the sort happened. This colossal swindle, imperial in its scope and claims, was now defended by the highest officials in the administration.

The claimants, under the name of the New England Mississippi Land Company, had infested the top reaches of the government, even, to Randolph's dismay, enlisting the postmaster general to become head of the company. The word went to the Congress: if you want post-office patronage, vote for the settlement of the company.

When the House Ways and Means Committee, Randolph's own, voted for what Randolph had exposed as a gigantic fraud, the Virginian leaped on his colleagues with all his peculiar fury. He unleashed this outburst on the Ways and Means Committee and by inference on the most powerful officials in the Jefferson administration:

> Sir, when the war-worn soldier of the Revolution or the desolate widow and famished offspring of him who sealed your independence with his blood, ask at the door of that committee for bread, they receive the Statute of Limitations. On such occasions, you hear of no equity in the case. Their claims have not the stamp and seal of iniquity upon them. Summum jus is the measure dealt out to them. The equity of the committee is reserved for those claims which are branded with iniquity and stamped with infamy.

Even those who were guilty were stung by this. And those who felt that they were voting for a practical compromise were as mad as hell at Randolph. The President brooded in the White House. While Jefferson probably could not have cared less if the swindlers were taken apart by Randolph's words, he pondered the greater problems that faced him. His own floor leader in the House attacked him and the administration in the kind of all-embracing attack that could not be assuaged by time or even apology (if that unlikely event ever were to take place). The President, possibly tired, surely irritated, came to the view that John Randolph, whatever his integrity of purpose, whatever his brilliance of thought and speech, was not the man to lead the Jefferson forces. Randolph, unhappily, was not a man to be swayed by party loyalty or administration policy. He said what he believed, and this is an irremediable flaw in an administration spokesman.

But it was the Talleyrand affair that snapped whatever threads bound the Jefferson administration to Randolph. Jefferson had been secretly sounding out Madrid to see if the Spanish government would be interested in selling the Floridas to the United States. The deal reached a stage at which Jefferson believed the sale was ready to be made. Suddenly it seemed to snag. The American agents of Jefferson in Spain could not locate the precise reason for the stalemate. Then, Jefferson learned that Talleyrand, the legendary foreign minister of Napoleon, had quietly, brazenly let it be known *sotto voce* to the Americans that if he, Talleyrand, were to find some good American money placed in his hand, the resistance in Madrid might be softened. It was outright bribery, but the Frenchman had imperial notions of how life ought to be lived, and his own poachings in France were not enough to keep him in the fleshy style that he enjoyed. So, then, the Americans should pay. It seemed so right.

Jefferson was tempted. To gather in the Floridas without a shot being fired, to buy this vast land acreage for a mere $2 million, and to have it all without a war, yes, Jefferson was sorely tempted. He decided that it was worth the gamble.

Obviously, Congress had to be consulted, but it had to be done with care and discretion. Jefferson, in a public message, indicated that the negotiations with Spain were still going on, and privately, very privately, he began to sound out the key members of the Congress, including, as it had to be, the irascible chairman of the Ways and Means Committee, Mr. Randolph of Virginia.

James Madison, the Secretary of State, was the chosen instrument for passing the news to Randolph. Whatever Madison's talents, his diplomatic skills, and his immense prestige, what he was selling was blackmail, and Randolph wasn't having any. He exploded when Madison's intent became clear.

But Jefferson was committed to the enterprise, seamy though it was, and thus the President summoned Albert Gallatin, the Secretary of the Treasury, and Randolph's closest friend in the administration, to persuade the volatile Virginian to sit tight and keep his mouth shut, an objective as impossible of attainment as bottling fire and flame.

Gallatin moved in on his friend, presented the need for secrecy and the possibility of great achievement at cheap cost. Randolph, outraged, sent him packing with no sliver of their intimacy remaining.

Whereupon Randolph, on the floor of the House, blew the cover on Jefferson's scheme. As one might have predicted, Talleyrand was disgusted with the bungling amateurs he was dealing with; he had had a higher opinion of the larceny quotient in the Americans, and, disappointed in his own judgment, he promptly axed the negotiations.

Randolph's harsh covenant with his own conscience shook the Jefferson administration, and it wobbled for a time; meanwhile, Florida remained in the grasp of Spain until 1817, when Andrew Jackson at the head of an intruding army fetched it from ineffectual Spanish hands. In either case, the United States had precious little principle to go on, but at least Jefferson's way was nonviolent.

The break between Jefferson and Randolph was now past any repair. Having cast off his administration moorings, now Randolph proceeded with an eerie zest for self-destruction to assault his other flank.

The fever for war in 1812 was at a delirious, heated pitch. Clay and Calhoun, brilliant, cutting, inexhaustible, were leading the war hawks, and the country, trembling with the premise of victory, was hard on their heels, willing to be led.

Randolph stood almost alone, thrusting, parrying, fending off the blows of Clay and his cohorts, and indeed, the temper of the country, for there was no longer any doubt of public sentiment in favor of a war.

Day after day, he rose in the House to lambaste the opposition, and in language that mounted and escalated in vehemence denounced the war hawks.

However, one day, he spoke with such bitterness that he overstepped himself, and severed the one bond that sustained him; he lost contact with his constituency. He said on that day:

> My friends, do you expect to find those who are now loudest in the clamor for war foremost in the ranks of battle? Or, is the honor of this nation indissolubly connected with the political reputation of a few individuals, who tell you they have gone too far to recede, and that you must pay, with your ruin, the price of their consistency?

The outrage leaped up against him in his home district, and hecklers gathered to attack him in the campaign in 1811. When some young toughs neared his platform, Randolph with no fleck of fear pointed at them, and said: "My Bible teaches me that the fear of God is the beginning of wisdom, but that the fear of man is the consummation of folly."

The administration sent in one of its ablest partisans into his district to oppose him. Randolph barely won. But when the war had been going for a year, and the populace gathered its patriotism and its support for the country's leaders, Randolph's undiminished sneers and blasts at the war effort finally did him in. He was defeated.

He came back to the Congress in 1815, but from this time forward, Randolph was like a rudderless raft, which drifted farther and farther away from where the practical problems of the Republic were being debated.

He was no longer consistent, he was rigid.

Perhaps he hated and believed too strongly. Perhaps his mind always teetered on those bleak edges where blank voids and fiery chambers receive those who fall over the side. A jury found him insane in 1821 after he had seemed for almost a year to be in a strange, unfathomable daze. He recovered.

Gerald Johnson places great importance on his early illness, and offers testimony by historian and physician alike to give circumstantial evidence that Randolph either had a congenital defect which caused him to be impotent or that the scarlet fever incident was the reason. He also suggests the validity of a study indicating that Randolph suffered from being a kind of "eunuchoid" in which unusual height, and growth of extremities, such as hands, fingers, and legs, are the results, and whose sources include among others severe cases of scarlet fever. All of this might explain in some measure the instability of Randolph and his violence of prose and manner.

Randolph, possibly, then resisted change because it would not have included him. He was stuck, irretrievably, with a foul aberration of Nature and God.

Perhaps, however, it was more likely that Randolph was the last idealist, the last politician to refuse to strike his guns because it was politic or practical to do so. "Change is not reform" was his famous battlecry, its sound running down the corridors of every conservative hall even to this day. He had no sight for American grandeur; he had no sense of national mission.

One is struck, constantly so, with the stand of Randolph and the creed of the new culturists, the young radicals of today. One may assume that time has a way of wiping out differences; the line marking the division between opposing philosophies has a way of skidding to the side, and those who might be on the right side of the line suddenly find themselves on the left. Theodore White, biographer of great presidential events, said: "The new culture [i.e., the 1970's] . . . deems any restraint on the expression of self as an abuse of liberty, and sees all government as the greatest repressor in the world." Give or take a minor accent, this is the selfsame credo of John Randolph, and if anything, he declared his aims more cruelly than the young dissidents of today. "I was not born to endure a Master," was Randolph's challenge to an enlarging federal authority.

He would have furnished the same answer to the ageless question as did the French businessman Legendre, when the great Gallic finance minister, Colbert, asked him in 1664: "What should we [the government] do to help you?" Legendre replied with the boldness of the physiocrats, "*Nous laisser faire*—let us do it, let us alone." Randolph's answer would have had more bite to it, more of a vinegary cutting edge, but it would have been the same.

Randolph was of the same piece as the French anarchist, Pierre Proudhon, who declared: "Whoever lays his hand on me to govern me is a usurper and a tyrant; I declare him to be my enemy."

He fought every change in constitutions, both state and federal, not because he found them flawless, but because he knew what they were, and he had no idea what kind of mischief new ones would bring.

(Randolph would have smacked the new radicals when they shout for bringing down what we have now without explaining what they have in mind to put in its place. But then Randolph might have become their leader, because he would have been the first to curse the government for intruding on what he always claimed was sacred personal liberty.)

Randolph put little trust in the manners of men. He knew that human nature was not unsoiled, and, though he and Jefferson were in agreement on few things, they understood the frailty of man. When he was in Paris, Jefferson wrote to Edward Carrington, and said: "If once the people become inattentive to the public affairs, you and I and Congress and Assemblies,

Judges and Governors, shall all become wolves. It seems to be the law of our general nature in spite of individual exceptions."

While Randolph might have placed less fidelity in the public's general intelligence, he would have surely seconded Jefferson's assessment of the human spirit.

The young modern radicals put much store in making love and not war, and entice themselves into a future shorn of hate and envy and greed and ambition. While they are vague about the structure they want to build, they do declare that it will be built around a community of spirit that denies all kinship with man's darker angels. It is this illusion that Randolph and Jefferson would have found fanciful, though each would have treated the solution differently. Randolph believed that the neighborhood, the city, the state would choose its own form of behavior, and that the national government could neither coerce the choice nor change the customs. Jefferson, on the other hand, encouraged "a little rebellion now and then" in order to keep in check the self-interests of those in power.

Thus, when Randolph assaulted Calhoun's support of Nullification as being utter nonsense, he was being true to himself, even though it seemed to be contradictory.

If a state were to stay in the Union, it had to obey the laws of the nation. Randolph held to the belief that from a stable society came the fruits and freedom for the society, and he found it stupid to cut away the very underpinnings of the stability which was the source of freedom. And yet, he could and did assail Jackson for his famous Nullification message, in which he threatened to put an army of soldiers right in the bosom of the South if that is what it was to take to keep legal sense among the Southerners. No federal government could coerce a state, said Randolph. Thus it was, this strange man always found himself alone in the center of the arena, circled by the growls and snarls of all those whom he had opposed, offended, and exposed.

Political discretion never resided in Randolph.

Late in his life, he put into a concise paragraph his philosophy of politics, which could be the lead chapter in the copybook of conservative maxims. Randolph said:

> I will vote against the amendment and on a principle which I had learned before I came into public life, and by which I have been governed during the whole course of my life; that it was always unwise, yes, highly unwise, to disturb a thing that was at rest. This is a great cardinal principle that should govern all wise statesmen—never without the strongest necessity to disturb that which is at rest.

Finally, he gave up on the country. It was going to hell, and there was no stopping place, no point where the grade downward would be eased. "The country is ruined past redemption by political and religious factions bidding at the auction of popularity where everything is 'knocked down' to the lowest bidder," he said one year before he died.

When it was all over, he was bitter, tormented, and old before he should have been. There was no place for him, no set of allies or any substantive issue to which he could give leadership with any possibility of triumph. He was alone, and unfriended by constituent or political comrade.

Randolph had no delusions about his form of political thought enduring. He was despondent about what would come hereafter in the Congress and in the country. What de Tocqueville described as "democratic despotism," the victory of a dull and intolerant mediocrity, probably fitted Randolph's inner instinct of tomorrow. He had no reason to believe that one generation could influence the next.

In a letter to a friend he said: "Of all the follies man is prone to, that of thinking he can regulate the conduct of others is the most preposterous."

But still he had one beside whom he could still stand: Edmund Burke. They were both critics of their society and its policies. They were both bearers of standards to which they repaired whenever they were under attack. They believed in a

Christian apparatus in which power is held in check by custom, and authority best employed by those who had the most to lose from ruin. Both Burke and Randolph had stern views about the tinkerer; to put here and take there to improve a constitution or a body of law was foredoomed to failure in their view, for political disciplines cannot be adjusted as one would a gear or a watch. The idea that one could redistribute wealth or purpose was both vicious and ludicrous to Randolph. "Remember, that property and power cannot be truly separated; if power be transferred to the propertyless, they will not remain long without property of some sort." It was the sort of statement that Polybius and Thucydides could have made about power and its corrupting influences on human nature.

Randolph was an anachronism before the word could even find roots in America. He put his faith in old ways and old habits. While it would be incorrect to say that today the radicals are nearer to Randolph than anyone else, it is fair to declare that Randolph's views on so-called "manifest destiny" and "America's mission" are fundamental to the antiestablishmentarians. Where the diverging takes place is in the detail. Randolph might say, if he could, that he fought with all he could bring to bear the coming of the kind of world which the revolutionaries despise and which Randolph foresaw with deadly clarity. Somehow he knew that he and old Virginia would have found the twentieth century graceless, neither to its taste nor to his.

DISRAELI:

THE "NEW POLITICS" LEADER

In a nation (indeed a world) confused about its future and presumably uncertain about its present, there is a reach for charismatic leaders who, with gaiety and stylish charm, will rectify our errors, lift our spirits, fill our voids, and lead us onto a higher level of "new politics" where student, intellectual, middle-class worker and assorted drab-humored and discontented masses will feel something akin to cheer.

Someone who can speak in epigrammatic jest, quote William of Ockham, enchant women, enthuse crowds, explain physiocratic philosophy, and sock it to 'em baby—this is the specification and, if the yearning is childish (according to the pols), it is nonetheless real (according to the polls.)

The very essence of this kind of leader appeared in nineteenth-century England. He was a Sephardic Jew, a popular novelist, a wit with talent, who became the headstone of Tory England, the prime exhibit of the peerage and the aristocracy, and who won in measure and endurance more affection from his sovereign than any other prime minister in all the catalogue of British history. Benjamin Disraeli bears more than passing resemblance to the hero-leader-charmer the Western world gropes for today.

He was the largest political talent of his age, with none but ordinary mortals on his side of the aisle in the Commons, and his departure from the parliamentary scene left his party intellectually insolvent. Even as he aged, the youth of England—the brilliant, the firebrands, the zealots—were mesmerized by him, and he by them. He welcomed youth, found pleasure in the young. "A party is lost," he said, "if it has not a constant reinforcement of young and energetic men."

His great rival was William Gladstone, who outlasted Disraeli in longevity, power, and public affection. This would not have surprised Disraeli, but it surely would have irritated him.

Not often in a nation's history do two such extraordinary leaders mount the parliamentary stage at the same time, dwarfing all those around them, living and jousting with each other in that icy, unpeopled zone where only the supremely talented find residence. There may have been other periods in the Anglo-Saxon political world when similar giants crowded the stage, the early days of the American Republic, England a hundred years before, when Pitt, Burke, and Fox were in full flower; but it is fair to say that Disraeli and Gladstone, so dissimilar in taste and purpose, so unfitted for tolerance of the other, so assured of the other's voids, and so confident of their own skill, were to light up the British Commons with a blaze of intellectual fire and gleam not to be repeated until Churchill stood alone a half-century later.

André Maurois juxtaposed these two with precise and telling accuracy:

> Disraeli's enemies said he was not an honest man. Gladstone's enemies said of him that he was an honest man in the worst sense of the word. Disraeli's foes said he was not a Christian; Gladstone's said he might be an excellent Christian, but that he was assuredly a detestable pagan. Disraeli was sure that Gladstone was no saint, but Gladstone was far from certain that Disraeli was not the Devil. Gladstone liked to choose an abstract principle and from that to deduce his preferences. And his tendency was to believe that his desires were those of the Almighty. He was reproached not so much for always having the ace of trumps up his sleeve as for his claiming that God put it there. Gladstone accepted as true all the cynical profes-

sions of faith which Disraeli made as a challenge; Disraeli put down as hypocritical the phrases by which Gladstone duped himself in good faith.

Once when Gladstone came out of the House after an adjournment, he was furious with some Disraeli remarks. "Sir," he bellowed at Disraeli, "you will come to your end either upon the gallows or of a venereal disease."

"That depends," answered Disraeli, "on whether I embrace your principles or your mistress."

Once someone asked Disraeli the difference between a calamity and misfortune. The famous sally, so often quoted, was: "Well, if Gladstone fell into the Thames, that would be a misfortune and if anybody pulled him out, that would be a calamity."

That was the Disraeli wit, and it was in debate and in conversation an instrument of awesome power. Perhaps in our day the zest for aphorism, the exquisite relish of the verbal harpoon, just the right shaping of phrase and moment calculated to devastate rival or ignoramus is no longer as desired or studied as it was in another time. If Disraeli were suddenly brought back to life today, only a politician of bottomless gall would challenge him to debate.

The odds are he would have chewed up William Buckley on television's "Firing Line" and spat him out, Yale sweater and all. ("I have observed, Buckley, that nothing seems to perplex you so much as an appeal to your honor.") One can imagine Disraeli on "Meet the Press" languidly countering one of Mr. Spivack's acidulous questions with: "My dear fellow, the low standard of American journalism is due to the fact that no television reporter has ever been shot to improve the craft."

In answer to a critic who claimed that Disraeli must be wrong, for he was so often castigated, Disraeli said: "He who anticipates his century is generally persecuted when living, and is always pilfered when dead." When he was told that his attacks on John Bright were too mean and that Bright was, to his credit, a self-made man, Disraeli laughed, and said: "Yes, I know he is, and he adores his maker."

His humor was always practical. When an associate gave Disraeli evidence that the aging Palmerston (for many years England's most durable first minister) was having a love affair with a married woman, Disraeli dismissed any thought of airing it. "Palmerston is now seventy," he explained. "If in his electoral address he could provide proof of his potency, he would sweep the country."

Sometimes he spoke with that odd sardonic candor that puzzled and unsettled both friend and enemy. After a session in the Commons where the Church of England was the subject and where Disraeli had risen to make his support of the established church known to his colleagues, he departed the meeting with his friend Walpole, to whom he said engagingly: "It is curious, my dear Walpole, that you and I have just been voting for a defunct mythology."

As he helped another member of the Commons into his coat after a particularly exciting session, Disraeli whispered into his friend's ear: "After all, we both know very well what brings you and me here: ambition."

Once when his own leader, the Tory prime minister Sir Robert Peel, changed from a protectionist (when he was in opposition) to a free trader (when he became prime minister), Disraeli rose to speak, addressing his remarks to the protectionist members of his party: "There is no doubt a difference in the right honourable gentleman's [Peel's] demeanor as leader of the Opposition and as Minister of the Crown. But that's the old story; you must not contrast too strongly the hours of courtship with the years of possession."

He had that gift of concise retort, saying it all and saying it deadpan. When all of England clamored for war against the Russians in their imbroglio with Turkey, Disraeli as prime minister was besieged with critics who fretted over his lack of martial spirit. Even the Queen was a hawk. Once, at a dinner,

Princess Mary of Cambridge sat next to him, and said (apropos of the delay in declaring war): "I cannot imagine what you are waiting for."

"At this moment, Madam, potatoes," answered Disraeli.

It was for his novels, which were all *romans à clef,* that Disraeli reserved some of his most potent shafts.

In the novel *Endymion,* Disraeli portrayed Palmerston in the guise of Lord Roehampton, who in the book is a ceaselessly energetic though aging Lothario. One of the characters remarks to Roehampton (Palmerston), "I cannot imagine a position more unfortunate than that of an exiled prince."

"Yes, I can," answers Roehampton. "To have the feelings of youth and the frame of age."

On the floor of the Commons, Disraeli was master. He was a professional, totally in charge of the complex procedures of the House and instantly knowledgeable of the labyrinth of debate. He battled all the great orators of the day, unattended by aides or colleagues, with either his skill or his courage, never faltering even in ill-health, always feared, often hated, never ignored.

Early in his career he took on Sir Robert Peel and destroyed him. It was done deftly, precisely, and with a surgeon's unerring eye for the right place to apply the scalpel.

It began rather inauspiciously. Peel rose to cut down this foppish young innocent. He used as his saber some lines uttered by a predecessor, Canning. The lines were apt and effective. But it was a dangerous game that Peel played, for he had done to Canning exactly what the Canning lines had reproved.

These are Canning's words, quoted by Peel:

> Give me the avowed, the erect, the manly foe,
> Bold I can meet,—perhaps may turn his blow!
> But of all plagues, good Heaven, thy wrath can send,
> Save, save, oh save me from the candid friend!

Disraeli did not reply at first. A few days went by. Then Disraeli spoke quietly, to protest against the system of appealing to the loyalty of the Tories in order to make them vote for Whig measures.

It is valuable to give Disraeli's reply, for no one can capture the luxuriant shatter of the retort without the actual words. Listen to Disraeli:

> The right honourable gentleman [Peel] caught the Whigs bathing and walked away with their clothes. He has left them in the full enjoyment of their liberal position and he is himself a strict conservative of their garments. [The House laughed uproariously. Peel sat somber.]
>
> If the right honourable gentleman may find it sometimes convenient to reprove a supporter on his right flank, perhaps we deserve it. I for one am quite prepared to bow to the rod, but really, if the right honourable gentleman, instead of having recourse to obloquy, would only stick to quotation, he may rely on it, it would be a safer weapon. It is one he always wields with the hand of a master; and when he does appeal to any authority, in prose or verse, he is sure to be successful, partly because he never quotes a passage that has not previously received the meed of parliamentary approbation, and partly and principally because his quotations are so happy.
>
> The right honourable gentleman knows what the introduction of a great name does in debate—how important are its effects and occasionally how electrical. He never refers to any author who is not great and sometimes who is not loved, Canning for example. That is a name never to be mentioned I am sure in the House of Commons without emotion. We all admire his genius. We all, at least most of us, deplore his untimely end. And we all sympathize with him in his fierce struggle with supreme prejudice and sublime mediocrity—with inveterate foes and with candid friends. The right honourable gentleman may be sure that a quotation from such an authority will always tell. Some lines, for example, upon friendship written by Mr. Canning and quoted by the right honourable gentleman. The theme, the poet, the speaker—what a felicitous combination! Its effect in debate must be overwhelming; and I am sure, if it were addressed to me, all that would remain would be for me thus publicly

> to congratulate the right honourable gentleman not only on his ready memory, but on his courageous conscience.

The House was in an uproar. It was a stunning achievement. Peel sat hunched in his seat, quiet, breathing heavily, deeply provoked, but determined not to reveal it, and deeply hurt, hurt beyond measure that this upstart should be so savage, so gaily malignant to the Prime Minister.

Some time later he attacked Peel again, even more cruelly. He spoke with telling effect, and the last twenty minutes of his speech were rapid-fire shots of invective and deadly sarcasm.

He described how the Peelites, "like the Saxons confronting Charlemagne were converted in battalions and baptised in platoons." He hit Peel savagely for his vacancy of mind and his use of other people's ideas. "His life has been one long appropriation clause. He is a burglar of others' intellect. There is no statesman who has committed political larceny on so large a scale." It was the most cruelly discomforting day of Peel's career. One month later, he was thrown out of office. Disraeli had pulled the great man down.

We are more polite today, at least in the clubby atmosphere of the cloakroom, the stump, and the TV studio. But the absence of ceremonial verbal assault may be due more to the diminution of the art of lethal reply than concern for the other fellow's feeling. The format of opposition today has been drained of any style. It is mostly formless, noisy, rowdy, and, if a good phrase has surfaced, it has gotten lost in the cluttered din from which it came.

Then there was the legendary Disraeli charm, always on exhibit when he chose it to be, a special powerful charm that all women found engaging, and most found irresistible.

Perhaps this unique quality, so voraciously sought by modern politicians, and unhappily for them too often beyond their ken, was visible in Disraeli because he *was* genuinely charming, as well as deeply committed to love of those he cherished. Nowhere is this on view more spaciously than in his marriage. Disraeli, sorrowfully, was forever in debt due to a continuous prodigality and a neglect of simple arithmetic. When he was thirty-five, he met and married Mrs. Wyndham Lewis, a rich widow, twelve years older than Disraeli, giddy, given to idiotic remarks, and with none of the social grace one would expect Disraeli to find attractive. The drawing-room gossip put it down to money-grubbing, and there was much buzzing of social tongues. But again, this odd, confounding man proved gossipers wrong. They were married for thirty-three years, a marriage to which Disraeli gave his total fidelity and from which Mary Anne, always sure of her husband's nearness and love, derived continuous happiness.

The story of Disraeli's long love for his older wife, that voluble, unsophisticated, even scatter-brained woman, is a chronicle of tenderness that defied all normal passion.

Mary Anne freed him from all the vexations of problems at home and the necessity of worrying about the important trivia of living, making it easy for him to relax, quietly and beyond the tumult of the jungle whence he came. She delighted in him, thought him a genius, and never considered any other motive worthy of pursuing except what Dizzy cared about or wanted. Few men would find this unattractive.

Her indiscretions of mind and tongue left him unperturbed. One day, one of Disraeli's closest supporters deigned to query him about a delicate subject. "Doesn't your wife's conversation annoy you just a little?" asked George Smythe.

"Oh, no, I am never put out by that," said Disraeli.

"Well, then," Smythe continued, "you must be a man of most extraordinary qualities."

Disraeli said: "Not at all. I only possess one quality in which most men are deficient: gratitude. She believed in me when men despised me."

When she died in her eighty-first year (Disraeli was sixty-eight), her husband was desolated. He was never the same man, and in the eight years left to him there was never again to be felt the security of soul and spirit that dwelled so long and with serenity within him.

Queen Victoria was not immune to Disraeli either. At first meeting, she found him strange; the sallow face, the curls, oiled and black, tousled over his forehead, the dandified dress he affected, bewildered and unsettled her. But soon, she was enchanted, and for all Disraeli's life he never had a more adoring friend than his Queen.

There is no question but what the relations between Victoria and her first minister were on a level and of a warmth that were unique. Disraeli always had some mesmeric rapport with women; his career shines with notable moments when women were the instrument through which his achievements in politics became possible. History is fat with messages, whispers, sonorous blends of chivalry and courtliness—and just plain, shameless flattery—that he sent to the various women who were his friends. There is no hint of the sensual or the forbidden in any of this, but only the irrepressible Disraeli charm working its magic.

In the last years of his life, when he was old and spent, the Disraeli charisma with the opposite sex never lost its spread. There is a story about a supper where young actresses and performers were present, and the question was put: "Whom would you rather marry, Gladstone or Disraeli?" The almost total response of the pretty girls was Disraeli, except one who answered: "Gladstone." When the others booed her, she cried: "But wait a minute, I would like to marry Gladstone so I could run away with Disraeli, just to see Gladstone's face!"

Victoria, like these young, beautiful girls, focused on Disraeli, and particularly after the death of her cherished Albert, she sought him out, lavished favors and attention on him. He wrote her notes and memoranda, surely unlike any that any prime minister ever wrote to a sovereign; they were gay, funny, using language as a supremely gifted writer would so employ it (many Englishmen never forgave the Fates for decreeing that their leader be a novelist and a witty one at that!). All the cultivation and knowledge and professional skill at telling a story that were part of the Disraeli intellectual baggage was poured in heaps at the Queen's feet. There were those who accused Disraeli of ladling all his buttery praise on a trowel, so thick did it pour. Disraeli shrugged this aside. When he was later asked the secret of his success with the Queen, he said quietly, even wistfully, "I never refuse. I never contradict. I sometimes forget."

This was, though, not exactly true. Disraeli never allowed the Queen to subject him to decisions he believed to be wrong; one, however, to which he grudgingly agreed but which he declared to be inexpedient was his support for the Queen to add to her titles that of Empress of India. He opposed her, for example, when she insisted on making the bishop of London the new archbishop of Canterbury. Disraeli remonstrated with her, gently saying at the end of his discourse: ". . . the Bishop of London sympathizes with everything that is earnest but what is earnest is not always true. On the contrary, error is often more earnest than truth."

The Prime Minister sent all his novels to his Queen. She sent him her *Journal of Our Life in the Highlands.* "Ah, Madam, we authors . . ." Disraeli would tell her with a smile.

Perhaps it was Disraeli's overpowering personal appeal that caused Victoria to despise Gladstone. Once the Queen revealed to intimates the source of the difference: "Gladstone speaks to me as if I were a town meeting, but Disraeli speaks to me as if I were a woman."

Disraeli was an activist, supremely confident of his gifts, who disciplined himself to enlarge his patience while he played second fiddle to the blue-blooded lords commanding the party. He exulted honestly when after so long a wait he finally assumed full power, and Sir William Fraser, in his *Disraeli and His Life,* recounts that when on February 27, 1868, he was formally installed in office, he said gleefully to friends who congratulated him: "Yes, I have climbed to the top of the greasy pole."

But it was a short-lived caretaker government he headed, and a few months later, without even waiting for Parliament to meet, Disraeli resigned. Gladstone, fresh from electoral victories, took over.

But in 1874, because Disraeli took particular care to fortify the Tory political organization, and because of an expanding unpopularity of Gladstone, the Tories smashed the Liberals at the polls and Disraeli began his only Downing Street tenancy of any length of time in the prime minister's office. He was seventy years old.

He was bold and full of courage, brandishing themes and causes where lesser, more cautious men would have hesitated or sniffed the public air before plunging ahead.

Nowhere is daring more visibly matched to energy than in his Suez coup, when with a stroke and a flair, he bought the interests of the Khedive in the Suez Canal Company. Not only did he secure the British life-passage to the East, but it was one of the most wondrously successful financial deals of all time. Disraeli paid four million pounds for the shares, and before 1914 they were worth forty million.

Since Parliament was not sitting when the opportunity arose, Disraeli had no funds. Undaunted, he sent a private emissary to the Rothschilds of London. "The prime minister wants four million pounds," was the request.

"When?" said Rothschild.

"Tomorrow."

"What is your security?" asked the banker.

"Mr. Disraeli said to tell you, 'the British government.'"

"You shall have the loan."

And that was the way it was done, or so the story goes. If it is somewhat apocryphal, those who admire Disraeli choose to believe it.

Issues change, but human nature does not. It is a piece of

irony that the same assets which Disraeli brought to the parliamentary stage in the mid-1800's in Britain would be congenially comfortable in twentieth-century United States. Fluency of tongue and mind, charm of phrase and movement, an actor's skill in presentation would have vaulted Disraeli from the 1868 Commons speakers' rostrum to the 1972 political television studio with only minor deterrents.

But he would also have brought with him the sobering certitude that pendulums never stand still, an axiom which societies, mayors, presidents, and revolutionaries must understand.

For all his skill and all his charm, at the very height of his power, when only so recently he was lionized by a grateful Queen and public, the Tory party was slaughtered at the polls, a total electoral defeat which, it appeared, no defense could have spoiled or baffled. Disraeli was flung from office, never to return.

If Disraeli had determined to hold an election when he returned from the Congress of Berlin, when he was hailed by Queen and populace as the savior of Britain, if he had quickly put his resurgence of favor to the voters, he would have had five more full years of power. But he felt comfortable, and reasoned that an election due to be held a little less than two years hence would give proof of his support.

However, there is an axiom of politics as true and steadfast in the middle years of the nineteenth century as it is today or was in the time of Pericles, and it is this: A nation forgets quickly the glory that it sought and applauded; it grows tired of citations of earlier triumphs and demands to know what fresh enticements are present. It is the incautious leader who believes in eternal gratitude from a public that finds the word rather curious in the first place.

It is also further evidence that in politics twenty-four hours is a very long time, that there is no such thing as "never" or "always" or "unbeatable." Those words are frivolously used by the naive and the excited, never by hard professionals.

The truth is that nothing is certain in politics, winning or losing, and this is so stable a truth that it can never be forgotten, though it often is. They had no polls in Disraeli's time, but in modern political life, no matter how furiously the computers clack out their cross-tabulations, whatever the polls say today is a worthless fig tomorrow, no more accountable to the future than a man's long-term health is to be judged by a horrible morning after the night before. The polls merely reflect a human condition, how the electorate feels at a specific moment, not how they will feel a month or a year hence.

Moreover, there is another maxim in politics, and it is this. The large issues defeat or elect presidents or prime ministers, not any momentarily exciting nitpick. Professionals know that the public has a pitifully short memory, for the public is a fickle wanton, capable of solecism and forgetfulness. There is a wanderlust in public anger. It ambles and thins and fades. The professional, being a practical animal and not given to try to change genetic heritage or rooted self-interests, uses this knowledge to let it work for him. The professional recognizes as few seem to that polls and current triumph or tragedy are of little importance, not very precious in gauging tomorrow, but are only brittle measures, fragile, blurred, and guilty of slovenly loyalty to a fixed cause or a certain person.

And the professional understands that timing is the indispensable linchpin to which every campaign is connected and on which every administration revolves. What happens a year before an election is a survivable injury. The same event occurring a week before the election can be a disaster (or delight, depending on whose ox is being gored).

In some quarters the name "political professional" has an odious meaning. It conjures up cartoons of fat, derby-hatted, cigar-smoking neanderthals passing out food baskets and voting the dead. That this image, possibly once true, has long since fled reality is overlooked, conveniently, by those who choose to have a target that is splendidly hittable. Political professional in the modern society, or at least as it is defined in this volume, means not the manager, the behind-the-scenes, non-elected administrator. It means the man in the arena, the candidate, the one who contends for public vote and favor. And when the description "professional" is placed in front of his name, it means precisely what the word intends: one who is consistently competent, who knows what he is about, does his homework, is instantly alert to promise and problem, is clearly sensitive to human nature and the interplay of issues and challenge as they mix in the public mind. And who possesses the crucial asset that separates the leader from the herd: instinct for decision.

The political professional is not afraid to lead, or to dare, or to challenge, but he is never so foolish as to get so far out front, or lag so far behind, that the people no longer believe him or follow him.

There is no school for this difficult education, except the school of actual experience. It is a mixture of intelligence and learning from mistakes, and the ability to judge a man or events or possible danger without clear proof of the judgment.

Some people are curt in their evaluation of the political pro. Usually these cynics are those who deal with politics as observers and not as participants, as counsellors and not as candidates, as philosophers and not as office-holders. To some of these people political issues must be dealt with as grand designs, the sum of what great expectations should create. They construct an idea or theory, give it the glory of fixed truth, and because it ought to be they expect it to be. But in the gritty dustbin of street politics what began as a beguiling theme can be washed away in a flash flood of public apprehension, public misunderstanding, and public discontent.

The political professional knows that the public must understand, the public must believe, the public must be incited to change, before the change can take place. This is the nub of professional leadership: the ability to sense the need before it is visible, and to insert into the public consciousness a willingness to experiment with something that is new in order to benefit the community.

While the professional applauds fresh new approaches to old problems, he is reluctant to mix personal theory with community reality. If the issue is key to the future, then it demands to be challenged and confronted in the long-range best interests of society. A problem can be solved, an issue raised, and a stand taken, but if the timing is wrong, success of the action can shatter against the real, hard edge of public disapproval. Thus, the professional puts his prestige and his pledge on the line only so often. He cannot waste what is so precious. He cannot enter the battle capriciously, whimsically.

The telling difference between the professional and the amateur is the swiftness with which they charge up the hill, banners waving, bugles tooting. Great causes are ofttimes dented and humiliated because someone sounded "Charge" before all the troops were ready to move. The professional may be wrong, but he is hardly ever guilty of stupid timing. And the ingredient which sets off the timing mechanism is that unfathomable and unplumbed apparatus called political instinct.

Unhappily for Disraeli, there was too much blind intellect and not enough political instinct present in his entourage.

The afterglow of Disraeli's supreme triumph at the Congress of Berlin, where his wit and iron will prevailed over those other leaders, including Bismarck, the toughest of them all; when Disraeli returned to Britain to assert that peace in Europe and Asia Minor was secure; when his powers were so obviously on the ascent and seemingly impregnable against all error, this afterglow was so strong that it is not so unusual that the unthinking and unprofessional Tory aides and party chieftains thought that even Fate itself could not intrude on the government's hold on its political tenure. What the Tory chieftains forgot about was luck, their lack of it, the Opposition's run of it, and the country's shortage of it. But then luck is as much a piece of valuable political baggage as precinct organization and issues.

Within months, there began an agricultural and industrial decline that sharpened in acceleration. As if this were not enough, disaster struck deep and hard in India, Afghanistan, and South Africa. That imperial policy which Disraeli had to such applause lifted up to Britain was now the petard on which the Tories, and the prime minister, hoisted themselves.

Lord Lytton, Disraeli's nominee as Viceroy of India, disobeyed Disraeli's orders, blundered, embroiled the Empire in a needless brawl at Kabul. Disraeli, vexed, grumbled: "When a viceroy or a commander-in-chief disobeys orders, he ought at least to be certain of success." But when the dice turn sour, all bets are in jeopardy. In South Africa another blunder by British proconsuls there brought about a terrible catastrophe when enraged Zulus massacred fifteen hundred British troops. Once again, in tight little corners of the world, the British lion was being mauled, and impolitely so. Perhaps, thought the people, Gladstone was right when he accused Disraeli of insane colonial policies. Just when Disraeli had determined that the pot was now simmering and all was under control again, the bad luck continued to run. The entire British mission at Kabul was assassinated. The ineptness of his lieutenants, who lacked the skill their chief so often made visible, was pulling the old man down. The last great political duel of the century was now fought between the two great political captains of their time.

All the Disraeli magic had run its course. All the splendor of past achievements so recently lauded now faded. In the election the Tories were wiped out in polling booths all over Britain.

Gladstone retrieved the prime ministership, to the distress of the Queen. When Gladstone came to call on her, Victoria, like many a monarch before her, was guided by hope rather than fact. She thought: "Mr. Gladstone looks very old and haggard, and his voice sounds feeble." When the ancient warrior murmured he did not expect to be in office long because of health, she was hopeful. It would have been too much of a blow to her to realize then that Gladstone's health was more robust than his opinion. For the next fourteen years he was a burly old lion, and took office again for the fourth time in 1892 at the age of eighty-two. It was ample proof that politicians are never completely credible in an assessment of their own durability.

All England felt the void when Disraeli died at seventy-six, on April 18, 1881.

The Queen wept. She wrote to Corry, his private secretary: ". . . I can scarcely see for my fast falling tears." Though protocol denied her the right to attend the funeral of one of her subjects (never to be violated until Elizabeth II went to the funeral of Churchill), Victoria could not abide her favorite first minister departing this earth without some personal embrace. Later, while out on a seemingly casual carriage ride, she caused his vault to be opened, and the sorrowing Queen laid a wreath of flowers on the coffin of her dear friend and most valuable guide. Never in the vast catalogue of British history has there been such love and loyalty between sovereign and statesman.

Disraeli was surely a nineteenth-century version of a new politics man. He was the first of the modern imperialists, and, by his own devising, he bound to the Tory party a middle-class support it could never have achieved without him. He did it by combining belief in the destiny of Britain abroad with social progress at home. He believed in the greatness of England and in the conviction that greatness sprang from the solid bedrock of the landed class. He would be out of joint with today's social trends, a kind of exotic inequalitarian. But it is no more valid to criticize Disraeli for his belief in the primacy of the English landed gentry than it is to ignore today the unequal odds that cause millionaires to have an increasing share of American national political victories.

We make noises about young men going into politics, but in the backroom every professional knows the spiraling costs of campaigning and the difficulty and the humiliation that are part of the money-raising process.

Since 1928, with the exception of Harry Truman, only grand heroes and men of wealth have held the presidency. The day of the poor rail-splitter type in the Senate is vanishing. Perhaps this may change, but it is an anomaly of our age that as our education widens and our freedoms enlarge, the politicians' arena narrows, beckoning mostly to men of property. Disraeli may be pardoned a smile, for in his own country since his leadership, there have been only two British first ministers, Lloyd George and Ramsay MacDonald, who neither inherited great wealth, nor went to a famous public school, nor attended one of the ancient universities.

His great idea was to give to the nation an intellectual and romantic ideal. He failed, in Maurois' opinion, because he was an aristocrat of the spirit, whereas the character of England was essentially that of its middle classes.

Disraeli would have found this view strange, since he would have described his leadership as one of liberalism in the finest Tory sense, and indeed one of generosity. He stirred with the notion that the ideas of *Coningsby* and *Sybil* (two of his early novels) could be given realistic form. From the first hours of his first ministry, he whipped through the Commons bill after bill to strengthen the life of the disadvantaged: equality of obligations between employers and employee; enlargement of the rights of trade unions; reduction of the hours of work to fifty-six in the week; half-holidays on Saturday; and a great many sanitation laws.

He had a splendid vision of Empire. He had a dream of an Imperial Parliament to whose chamber would come from the far-swept corners of the globe all those representatives of Her Majesty's lands, and in this chancellery girdled round with diversity and change there would be found unity and pride, not only in the Queen and her Crown, but in the indissoluble bond of fraternity that was the outer skin of the imperial palm.

There was much to fault in Disraeli. He was too vain. He was not above deception when it came to personal finances. He tugged too often at the doors of the great houses whose estates he found so attractive. He could, when events collided with his ambition, rise above principle. But he had a conception of his country that he believed to be right.

At a later time, there would surface in Winston Churchill that latter-day dream of Disraeli, and if it did not even yet find its secure rooting, at least it was to live in another prime minister who believed, as did Disraeli, in the mystical bonds that bound together the British destiny. (The historian J. H. Plumb was later to criticize Churchill harshly for what he considered to be Churchill's old-fashioned notion of a British connection with some divine right of supremacy.) Disraeli and Churchill believed alike that their island kingdom was not some abstraction, logically conceived and arithmetically wrought. They counted it a work of art, tempered by pain and constructed by men who believed that the greatness of England was extracted from the institutions that endured through all the years before. Or, as Maurois pointed out, "the rights of Englishmen are older by five full centuries than the Rights of Man."

Disraeli had a belief in Fate, not only for his country, but for himself. He had no occasion to doubt his own unique gifts, and he exploited them to the fullest when the time had come. He often quoted a maxim of Cardinal de Retz: "Everything in the world has its decisive moment; the crowning achievement of a good conduct of life is to know and pick out that moment."

"What is the most desirable life?" someone asked Disraeli when he was very young. And Disraeli answered with all the fire that was ready within him: "A continued grand procession from manhood to the tomb."

But it truly came too late for Disraeli. He was old, his stamina had fled when finally he became chief arbiter of his nation's destiny. One may speculate what might have been if he had been born in some great old castle, to a landed family rich with titles and wealth, and had free rein to leap on top at an early age. Churchill mused on this dereliction in his memorable book *Great Contemporaries,* and when writing about Joseph Chamberlain he said: "The amount of energy wasted by men and women of first-class quality in arriving at their true degree, before they begin to play on the world stage, can never be measured. One may say that sixty, perhaps seventy percent of all they have to give is expended on fights which have no other object but to get to the battlefield."

How sadly true about Disraeli. Beaten four times in an attempt to get into Parliament, an odd, strange figure, his origins, his appearance, his lack of social connections and family wealth all conspiring against him, he set forth on his climb, fighting a hundred battles on his way to the battlefield.

He was indeed alone, armed only with his talent, his awesome eloquence, intelligence, and that animal instinct which all great leaders must have which tells them with the exactness of a metronome when to strike and when to withdraw.

Before the Queen ever really got to know Disraeli, she complained to Lord Stanley, Disraeli's party chief, about the savagery of Disraeli's assault on Peel. "I do not approve of Mr. Disraeli and I do not approve of his conduct," said the Queen.

And Stanley answered with a perception of truth and wisdom: "Madam, Mr. Disraeli had to make his position and men who make their positions will say and do things which are not necessary for those for whom positions are provided."

Disraeli spent his life at the bottom and lower levels of that Greasy Pole, and only in the late time of his age did he finally achieve that summit to which so much of his efforts had for so long been directed. How many years was it, then? For only eleven out of thirty-five years after 1846 was he in any kind of office and of those, five years were in governments with brief tenancy and only five and a half years in the prime minister's office, where for the first time he was able to move unburdened by the heavy weight of social superiors who were not of the intellectual quality of the one who was for so long their lieutenant.

Does anything remain of Disraeli's influence? Walter Bagehot wrote of him two years before he was thrown out of office for the last time that "though he had charmed Parliament he never did anything more. He has no influence with the country."

Robert Blake, who has explored the Disraeli life and legend with more perspicacity than almost anyone else, finds him a "timeless figure," one who would operate with ease today or a century earlier than his own time. He was both skeptic and romantic. According to Blake, he was "less optimistic about the extent to which human endeavor could improve the lot of humanity. The spirit of strenuous moral effort, belief in progress, confidence in material prosperity struck no echo in his mind. 'Progress to what and from where' said Disraeli."

There was much of the oriental in Disraeli. He had a curious double vision, the ability to sense the need for the good things for himself and others, and an instinct for their emptiness.

In many ways he was a contradiction. His manner and mannerisms were indeed strange to the times, and they put people off. It was not the first time, nor the last, that a man had to pay for the externals of personal style as contrasted with the grit and substance of achievement. And yet Blake views that very style as the essence of his durability. He was, says Blake, the superb presenter, the great parliamentarian. "He knew how small a part in politics is played by logic, cool reason, calm appraisal of alternatives. This is why politicians appreciate him. They realize that a large part of political life in a parliamentary democracy consists not so much in doing things yourself as imparting the right tone to things that others do for you or to things that are going to happen anyway."

Perhaps this is true. If it is, should it be? But it is true, as Blake points out, that much of the art of politics consists in shadowing behind a shield of principle and philosophy those maneuvers and twists in the road that events over which presidents and prime ministers have little control force upon them. Finally, he was a candid man (when he chose to be), on whom today's press might lavish some of their interpretative glory, for he was "good copy." He deprecated noble aims (even his own) with caustic satire and that inevitable irony with which he clothed even the most painful thrusts. "The people have their passions and it is even the duty of public men occasionally to adopt sentiments with which they do not agree, because the people must have leaders."

Disraeli always knew what the indispensable ingredient was (in his time as it is in ours), for he admired it in others as he gathered it within himself. Shortly before his death, he wrote to the daughter of Robert Salisbury, his foreign minister and later prime minister: "You will find as you grow older that courage is the rarest of all qualities to be found in public men. Your father is the only man of real courage that it has ever been my lot to work with."

This Glorious Company

THE MEN WHO BUILT THE CONSTITUTION, PHILADELPHIA, MAY TO SEPTEMBER, 1787

Within the single twelve-month period of 323 to 322 B.C., Athens suffered the deaths of her greatest orator, her greatest philosopher, and her greatest ruler; Demosthenes died at sixty-two, as did Aristotle at the very same age, and Alexander. The rupture of the Greek era had begun, and some historians say that this year ought to be singled out as the ancient world's most sorrowful moment.

On the other hand, Edward Gibbon fixed the span of time when the "condition of the human race was most happy and prosperous" as that period from the accession of Nerva as emperor of Rome in A.D. 96 until the death of Marcus Aurelius in A.D. 180.

It is quite possible that in America a single moment could be chosen that would pinpoint the death of one period and the beginning of another. On July 4, 1826, several hundred miles apart but within hours of each other, John Adams and Thomas Jefferson died. A coincidence of tragedy that strains credulity and truth, it is a strange piece of business that these two men, who so fitted together in the birth of a nation, should breathe their last on the fiftieth anniversary of the Declaration they so mightily created and for so long and with such fidelity defended and enlarged. No wonder that the chroniclers should call that hour in 1826 a monument to God's odd command, and a moment for large national grief.

Possibly there should be no quarrel with either historian or patriot who classifies eighty-five days of constitution-making in 1787 as the most momentous slice of history in the American past.

The story of this creation of a civil authority on a scale never before imagined is the drama of human capacities stretched to the outer edge, and the congealing of splendid idea and pragmatic instinct into something which for almost two hundred years of cruel disjointing has survived, and prospered.

For the second time in the history of Western man there was to be a gathering of a national leadership to write down rules for nationhood, in which restraining boundaries were to be spelled out. The first time this was done was at Runnymede in a meadow outside London, where vexed landed barons forced a frustrated King John to sign the Magna Carta. The Great Charter, a string of sixty-one clauses knitted together without arrangement or order, set forth how sovereign and subject ought to get along. In a sense, the Great Charter said to the King: "Get your heel off my neck, and we can live together, you on your throne, and we on our estates."

The defect of the Magna Carta was well known to the men at the Constitutional Convention. They were all too aware that the Charter, while revealing the sources of discontent and even regulating its reshaping, had no sanction of law or force to keep the King respectful of its clauses. In short, the Magna Carta was a toothless indictment, and as soon as John and his heirs got free of the barons' broadsword they went back to their old ways, which is to say they ignored the Magna Carta.

Now once again, some five hundred and fifty years later, another group of men, of the upper class like the barons, determined to write its own charter of self-regulation.

The "why," the "what," the "how," and the "who" of the making of the Constitution is the drama. The characters could not have been more perfectly cast, except for the absence of two great talents of the age, Jefferson and Adams.

Let us understand why the Convention was called to devise a constitution.

The states were being governed by the Articles of Confederation, a curious amalgam of clauses and faiths (like Magna Carta), having no power at all either to force the states to bend to the national will or to employ any means of collective action against men or states who determined to defy the Congress. Written in 1776 to 1777, ratified on March 1, 1781, the Articles were the bricks, loosely mortared, that bound the states together. The states retained "sovereignty, freedom and independence." Officeholders held nothing but the office. The Congress could make treaties, but the states did not have to honor them. The Congress could construct an agreement in foreign trade, but could not regulate it nor collect taxes on it; it could put out a call for money, but had no force to collect it; it could borrow money, but had no means to repay it; and it could print money, but could not support it. The Articles crippled the government; it limped, and swayed, and had trouble breathing, and yet it was the living pillar on which the entire nation must lean. There was much in the Articles that later found its way into the Constitution, but the single most frustrating omission in the Articles was the lack of coercive power granted to the federal government, and on this vacancy the young victorious colonies foundered when the war ended.

General Washington, the grim, silent father figure of the colonies, and the one man in all the states who collected the respect, the awe, and the admiration of the various leaders, knew from the bitter tea of inefficiency he drank all during the war that the Articles were a sham. No respectable government could rise from its rostrum, indeed no nation could lay a claim to the future whose thrusts and hopes were tangled in a feckless charter which encouraged individual states to go their own way. Sure enough, as soon as the war ended, brawls between the states became endemic: one state taxed another; there were quarrels about fisheries, land boundaries, debts were in confusion. Even the dullest of colonists knew that something was amiss.

At this juncture, perhaps the most extraordinary man produced in the United States began to jostle the conscience and the energy of the nation. Alexander Hamilton is one of those astonishing children of nature who springs unheralded from misty beginnings, brimming with some magic, galvanic fury, in whose brain and spirit flowed some unmeasured and unduplicatable intelligence. One can only surmise "what might have been" had he not been cut down by Aaron Burr's bullet. Beginning in 1780 (he was twenty-three years old), he pushed, shoved, cajoled, wrote, implored, and exerted a cold, insistent logic, on the premise that if the colonies were to survive, they must organize a strong government.

As the Articles proved less enduring, Hamilton won over more of the elite of the land. Virginia's men, quarreling with Maryland, enlarged a meeting with their neighboring state into what became the famous Annapolis Commission of September, 1786, attended by delegates from five states, including the restless, prodding Hamilton. Together with James Madison, Hamilton seized the chance, and the Annapolis Commission issued a call for all thirteen states to "devise such further provisions as shall appear to them necessary to render the constitution of the federal government adequate to the exigencies of the Union."

Meanwhile, there occurred another event, violent, brutal, and sad, but which in an odd and eerie fashion caused the propertied men of the colonies to seriously inspect the need for a more stable government for the future.

In the fall of 1786, mobs of western Massachusetts farmers, angrier than they had ever been, bullied their way into the courtrooms and prevented the judges from executing instruments to collect debts and taxes. They were broke, weary, and had their fill of some dude tax collector taking away what they rightfully claimed as their own. (It is another strange piece of business that men like Samuel Adams proposed to hang anyone who used the same violent means that he employed against the British in 1774. Substitute college students for farmers, and congressmen and university presidents for Sam Adams and the revolutionary leaders of 1776, and you have a modern-day picture of the torment of western Massachusetts.)

The governor of Massachusetts called out the militia to halt these assaults on the courts. A man named Daniel Shays, an obscure farmer who had served with valor in the war as a captain in a Massachusetts line regiment, became, probably against his will, the leader of the mob. He was poor, hopelessly in debt like his fellows. He could not even raise twelve dollars to pay off an obligation he owed.

The militia took up positions to defend the courthouse and the arsenal at Springfield, and with 1,100 men armed with artillery, the militia broke the back of the insurgents at this skirmish. On February 7, 1787, a new army of militia, led by General Benjamin Lincoln of Revolutionary War fame, pursued the mob and scattered them with heavy losses. Captain Shays escaped to Vermont. Providentially, the state government of Massachusetts swallowed its rage, pardoned all the leaders with brief prison terms, and the newly elected legislature (generally in sympathy with the rebellious farmers) granted some of their demands, such as allowing notes of the soldiers-now-farmers to be tendered for taxes.

But the shock of the insurrection leaped like the tip of a flame throughout the colonies. When Massachusetts appealed to the confederation for aid and assistance, the Congress was unable to do one thing. General Washington soberly confronted what he chose to believe was a practical and indispensable move, to gird a new government with power to act and tax and govern.

Washington was concerned about "the combustibles in every state." He said: "I feel . . . infinitely more than I can express . . . for the disorders which have risen." "The American war is over," wrote an obscure citizen of New Jersey, "but this is far from being the case with the American Revolution . . . it remains yet to establish and perfect our new forms of government."

John Adams was more right than he possibly could have known, when he said that from the beginning he had seen more difficulty from our attempts to govern ourselves than from all the fleets and armies of Europe.

It may have been a spur to the tenacity of some of the framers of the Constitution that they had suffered at the hands of mobs, men like James Wilson of Pennsylvania, Robert Morris of Pennsylvania, John Dickinson of Delaware. Most of the leaders in the colonies were committed to finding some way of governing themselves but without either a monarch or anarchists charting the course. Men who had been witness to mob rule and crowd hysteria were the keenest to build something sturdier.

The leadership in each of the states pondered the significance of the farmers' war, and it is fair to say that every leader in every state was influenced by the portent of the rebellion. Only in the legation at Paris, where Thomas Jefferson represented his young nation, did there emerge an unlikely view of Shays's Rebellion.

Jefferson wrote to Abigail Adams: "The spirit of resistance to government is so valuable on occasion that I wish it to be always kept alive. It will often be exercised when wrong, but better so than not to be exercised at all." In another letter to Abigail's son-in-law, William Smith, Jefferson wrote the words that revolutionaries from that time forward have taken as their testament and incentive to intrude on organized civil authority: "God forbid we should every twenty years be without such a rebellion! What signify a few lives lost in a century or two? The tree of liberty must be refreshed from time to time with the blood of patriots and tyrants. It is its natural manure."

Thus it was that a confluence of intellectual force and an insurgent group of penniless farmers cleared the way for a colonial will to construct a federal authority of self-government. Alexander Hamilton, James Madison, and Daniel Shays make an odd trio, but then history has a way of disguising great events with a comic turn.

There now remained, however, the "what" of the Convention. What were the obstacles that crowded their every step, and which threatened from the very outset to demean the proceedings and choke the Convention into lassitude and failure?

The three great barriers were very clear to all. First, there was the issue of slavery and how to handle it. Second, there was the problem of representation in the Congress, small state versus large state, and how to compromise it. And third, there was the matter of the chief executive, his term, his powers, and his office and how to shape it.

There were other problems, large, inconvenient, seemingly unsolvable, but these three captured the immediate interest of the delegates, and on their solution raged the running battle that struggled without intermission through a hot summer in Philadelphia.

The story of how they were resolved and who were the major instruments in the agreement is really the greatest dramatic confrontation in the building of the newest nation, soon to become the most powerful nation, acting under a rubric of written authority that at this hour is the longest-lived such government in the world.

The "how" of this story is an exercise which ought to be required reading for every young person, whether he be idealist, radical, or apathetic observer, for in the "how" of the Constitution—how it was put together, how gross misunderstanding and hostile views were examined, and polished and merged—is the classic case study of agreement under pressure, of an intellectual give-and-take whose influence on succeeding generations cannot be measured except by the endurance of the result.

The "who" of the Convention is the roll call of the best the colonies could offer. Though it is true that some of the finest brains were absent, it is also true that the collection of men who assembled in Philadelphia beginning May 25 was both a conclave of excellence and a microcosm of the young nation—no, that is not entirely true, for the men of Philadelphia could not have been part of a modern, carefully hewed sample of the socioeconomic universe our scientific poll takers are fond of constructing. There were no poor farmers and settlers on hand; there were no slaves; there were no shopkeepers and tenants of the huge estates. It must be truthfully reported that those who reported to Philadelphia were the elite of the land, those immense figures of finance, politics, war, and ideas, whose names, by and large, were as well known to the colonies as those of modern-day leaders.

Finally, on February 21, 1787, the Congress invited the states to send delegates to a convention at Philadelphia in May "for the sole and express purpose of revising the Articles of Confederation. . ." (That one sentence proved to be an unruly piece of prose, for it pitted the pro-Constitution men against the anti-Constitution men; whether to "revise" the Articles or to abandon them totally for a new and fiercely strong new document. The first fundamental and far-reaching decision in the Convention was the majority view that a new charter had to be created, and the Articles abandoned.)

Seventy-five delegates were named to the Convention. Fifty-five showed up. Even so, no more than eleven states were represented at any one time, and no more than thirty delegates were present at any given meeting.

Two (Johnson and Baldwin) were college presidents; three (Wythe, Wilson, and Houston) were or had been professors; twenty-six others were college graduates. Nine were foreign-born, four had read law at the Inns of the Court of London. Forty-two had served in the Congress, and most of the others in the state legislatures. More than half were lawyers, eight were merchants and traders, five were planters, three physicians. Seven had been governors of their states, twenty-four had fought for their country's independence as officers in the Continental Army, or in their respective state militias. At least one half of the delegates owned Negro slaves.

The average age was just over forty-three. Three were under thirty years old: Jonathan Dayton of Ohio was twenty-seven, John Francis Mercer of Maryland was twenty-eight, Richard Dobbs Spaight of North Carolina was twenty-nine. Alexander Hamilton was thirty; Madison, thirty-six, Gouverneur Morris, thirty-five, and Edmund Randolph, thirty-three. James Wilson, Luther Martin, Oliver Ellsworth, and William Paterson were between forty-one and forty-five. General Washington was fifty-five, John Dickinson, fifty-four, and George Wythe, sixty-one. Only four members had reached or passed the age of sixty. Benjamin Franklin was the oldest at eighty-one.

Three had been in the Stamp Act Congress, seven had signed the Association of the First Continental Congress, six had signed the Articles of Confederation, eight had signed the Declaration of Independence, and it must be said that five others were cheated of this honor because they were fighting in the war. At least thirty had done some kind of military duty, and half that number could have been said to have been toughly experienced in battle.

(Roger Sherman of Connecticut was the only member of the Continental Congress who signed all four of the great American state papers: the Declaration of 1774, the Declaration of Independence, the Articles of Confederation, and the United States Constitution.)

Most of all, the men of Philadelphia were scholars, men of ideas, who from their earliest beginnings were cognizant of and conversant with the sages and the prose and the philosophers of the Western world. Mainly, they were of the liberty-oriented political philosophies, the school of natural law and natural rights.

They had read deeply and absorbed much. Indeed, their principal baggage was books. Jefferson, for example, shipped to Madison and Wythe from Paris sets of Polybius (that ancient who first set forth the idea of separation of branches of government, later to be enlarged by Montesquieu).

The dimensions of the delegates' knowledge of the political works of the time is a spectacular measure. In the writing of the treason clause in the Constitution, the delegates made it perfectly clear that they were intimately familiar with the statutes of Edward III written in 1351, and lifted that ancient examination of treason almost verbatim from its dusty rolls and inserted it in their own document.

The educated men of the Convention were as well versed in political history and political theory as they were fully knowledgeable of the literature of classical Greece and Rome.

When Madison was a member of the Continental Congress, he prepared a reading list of books "proper for the use of the Congress." It is a remarkable catalogue. He included Hume, who, according to historian Irving Brant, "exposed the misdeeds of conservatives in apologizing for them"; Clarendon, a Stuart royalist; the two iconoclasts Rapin-Thoyras and Kennett, who said quite nasty things about kings and their assumption of divine rights. Also on the list were two storehouses of sticks and stones to hurl at royal ministerial oppressors—*Cabala: Mysteries of States, in Letters of the Great Ministers of King James and King Charles,* and Rushworth's *Historical Collections,* an eight-volume discourse whose endless probings were required reading for the cultivated colonial gentlemen. There were volumes of Sidney, Locke, Harrington, and Priestley, as well as Hobbes and Seldon, and of Justinian, Coke, and Blackstone; the Italian Beccaria, who aroused Europe to the terrors of torture and the compulsory forms of self-incrimination; Burnet's *History of My Own Time,* which told among other tales the squalid episode of Titus Oates, that formidable liar, and the lamentable joining of informers, perjurers, and cheats whose "testimony" sent many an English Catholic to his death.

The singular aspect, then, of the delegates to Philadelphia was their broad and full political vision, sharpened by a truly vast knowledge of the thinking available in the world. It may be accurate to state that no political assembly before or since has contained this amount of comprehension and awareness of such a variety of written thought.

It may also be fair to say that no other group of political shapers were better acquainted with the incendiary philosophers of their time. A colonial Un-American Activities Committee would have a zesty field day with the delegates' libraries.

It was the opinion of Horace White that the Constitution of the United States "is based on the philosophy of Hobbes and the religion of Calvin. It assumes the natural state of mankind is a state of war, and the carnal mind is at enmity with God."

This view is essential to any understanding of this assembly of uniquely endowed and cultivated men—as is a recognition of what they were not, as certainly as we must know them for what they were. They were not starry-eyed idealists lifting up their hopes for a perfect apparatus of government. Though they prefaced their final document with an importuning for "a more perfect union," they plainly were trying to cajole a Divine Being for something better than they had, not the flawless mechanism which they knew could never be achieved.

In truth, they were not democrats in the literal sense. They were an elitist corps of propertied men, a little frightened by the rabble of arms in the outer edges of their new land, queasy over the prospect of anarchy, unsure of the "people," and determined that while there must be freedom it must also be checked and reined in with a system of orderly arranged political baffle-plates, not easily rumpled and hospitable to quick repair. What they had won at great risk in a long war, they were not prepared to fritter away in a casual lawlessness.

The American revolt may have been the only rebellion in history stirred, organized, and led by the wealthiest, the most intelligent, and the most civilized among the rebels. There was much talk among these leaders about the unfitness of the common people to take any participatory role in government:

Elbridge Gerry spoke of democracy as "the worst of all political evils." Roger Sherman urged that "the people have as little to do as may be about the government." William Livingston declared: "the people have ever been and ever will be unfit to retain the exercise of power." And General Washington in what may have been the first call to politicians to be true to themselves rather than to the voters, said: "If to please the people, we offer what we ourselves disapprove, how can we afterward defend our work? Let us raise a standard to which the wise and the honest can repair; the event is in the hand of God." If Washington seemed a bit less reproving of the capacity of the people to govern themselves, he was as leery as the rest of their desire for excellence.

These men of substance and philosophic depth were not gathered together to construct a social engineering document. They were assembled to design and build a political edifice. In this latter time, when the social sciences are so important in the political landscape, it is important to understand that there were no such hang-ups in Philadelphia. The men of the Convention were hung up on the slavery question only insofar as it obtruded on the population count. While there were abolitionists present, there was no compulsion to fight and die on the slavery issue; indeed, it never came close to that. Slavery was recognized as part of the organic structure of the nation, and indentured servants had no Horatius standing at any bridges. Thus, no imaginative breakthrough was attempted to erase the stain of slavery, but, rather, an agreement on a truncation point after which it would be illegal to import new slaves. It is no indictment of these men to describe them as having no problems whatever in considering slaves as property; in truth their conscience troubled them and made them know that slavery was wrong, indecently and oppressively wrong.

In spite of this, however, every man present believed that this issue would have wrecked the Convention if it had been allowed to surface. Their first priority, over which no moral or legal obstruction was allowed to prevail, was to build a workable government. That the first compromise that took place which assured the continuation of the meeting also foredoomed succeeding generations to a bloody, fratricidal conflict would not have swayed the delegates. They were willing to exalt their priority at the expense of a delayed time bomb. Consider that nowhere in the Constitution does the word *slave* or *slavery* even appear. At four scattered points in the Convention, it is euphemistically referred to, always masked in fuzzied words. The price of a ratified Constitution was the sacrifice of an honorable, swift end to slavery. One must count with his own gauge if the price were too high, or whether it should have been paid at all.

This is the great tragedy of the Constitution. It is not enough to say that slavery should have been clearly and totally denounced, and expunged from the land. The vacancy, filled with blood and bitterness some seventy-four years later, was there, and only fitful attempts were made to cover it up.

If there could have been said at the Convention, "Gentlemen, if we don't attack this cancer now, this nation will fight the meanest, bloodiest war in all its history and will very likely destroy itself," if someone had said that, and meant it, would the delegates have acted any differently? Perhaps it would have depended on the man who said it. If Washington had commanded the floor and with his grave and severe fury had demanded a choice to be made, perhaps, just perhaps the delegates might have responded. But most historians probably would be gloomy about the outcome of such a hypothetical confrontation. At any rate, no one said it. This, then, was the stain of the great document, and from this omission there flowed misery in abundance, and desolation and schisms that to this hour are not entirely healed, if indeed, they ever will be. But the thought is incandescent: *If* the delegates could have spent their anger in debate and finally agreed on the abolition of slavery, what might have been? But the incandescence fades and the blot remains.

What this proves is that even in the best of assemblies, where only the most thoughtful and the wisest convene, there is the possibility of error. No man is flawless and no man ought to be accounted as such by anyone—his students, his followers, his family, or his nation. Whenever a political leader, or an academician or a philosopher or whoever, rises to testify that what he thinks and says bears the divinity of unshakable truth, he ought to be immediately suspect. The arrogance of certainty was as present in the Constitutional Convention as it is on view in too many college faculty rooms, in too many legislatures, state capitols, and in the House and Senate and White House, too.

The best one can say about the men of Philadelphia is that while they never announced their error of omission on slavery, they did at least hasten to repair what they had so negligently laid aside when they failed to establish the full embrace of civil liberties. Thus, they restored in the Bill of Rights what they had failed to do in the original framing of the Constitution. Perhaps they would murmur and say that they were so concerned with the political shaping of their governing machine that they just plain forgot to examine its potential to oppress. In any event, they did, in a way, declare they made a mistake, and they made it right.

But within this body of constitutionalists, there was an accumulated wisdom that in the end of it all was the sustaining influence in the summation of the final document. With all the wealth and the tendency toward the interests of commerce, the movement of the Convention was always toward the aspirations of what we would call today the "common man." George Mason reflected the general view of the more spacious-minded liberals in Philadelphia when he said: "Notwithstanding the oppression and injustice experienced among us from democracy, the genius of the people is in favor of it, and the genius of the people must be consulted."

Madison, in *The Federalist* number 51, perhaps capsuled the ultimate aim of the framers when he wrote: "If men were angels, no government would be necessary. In framing a government which is to be administered by men over men, the great difficulty lies in this: you must first enable the government to control the governed, and in the next place oblige it to control itself."

And Hamilton, when he spoke to the ratifying convention in New York, perhaps underscored the intent of the Constitution (Hamilton's view is pertinent, for, as all students know, there was no larger advocate of an aristocratic cabal) when he said: "Men will pursue their interests. It is as easy to change human nature as to oppose the strong current of selfish passions. A wise legislator will gently divert the channel, and direct it, if possible, to the public good."

No enterprise like the making of the Constitution, infected with the passions and dogmatism and idealistic reach of fifty-five individualistic men, can escape either scrutiny or criticism. Charles Beard, in 1913, with his *An Economic Interpretation of the Constitution of the United States,* was the first credible historian to be critical of the Founding Fathers. He set up a view of the men of Philadelphia as crabby old conservatives bent on holding onto their own estates to the exclusion of those without. But Beard himself, in later appraisals, admitted that the delegates were remarkably scrupulous in their moderate and honest aims, and, if any proof is needed at all, the ultimate script they prepared and signed is ample evidence of their skill at political architecture and governmental carpentry. What they built had its pilings fastened deeply in a solid foundation. Endurance is possibly still the most valid guarantee of excellence.

It is Clinton Rossiter's judgment that the four principal influences in the Convention were James Madison, George Washington, James Wilson, and Gouverneur Morris.

Madison and Wilson intruded into the very heart of the Convention. No issue escaped their razor's edge. No problem found its way to light and agreement without their guiding hand.

General Washington's contribution was of a different and, in many ways, an essential kind. His very presence was indispensable. He loomed over every session, always there, silent, immovable, surely implanted in the minds of every framer as the first chief executive. He made but one speech in all the harassing, tedious, interminable debates of the Convention, rising on the last day to speak quietly about the proposition which intended to change the ratio of population to representation. He spoke briefly, and, when he had finished, the old patriarch took his seat. The Convention took the vote and sustained their leader.

Morris, a sardonic, witty, clever man, maintained a steady flow of work in committee and earned the widespread respect of his conferees. Forty years later, Madison spoke of Morris: "To the brilliancy of his genius he added, what is too rare, a candid surrender of his opinions, when the lights of discussion satisfied him, that they had been too hastily formed and a readiness to make the best of measures in which he had been overruled." It is a capsule description which one might hope would be sought out and worn by other leaders.

At the outset, the Convention built two safeguards which set the form and tone of the meeting and without which it is difficult to catalogue the possible alternative results.

The first was secrecy.

On May 28, with a quorum of delegates present, the Convention with common consent bound itself to public silence. The records of the meeting were to be inviolable. The delegates could not absent themselves without permission, and nothing spoken in the chamber could be repeated outside.

In the twentieth century, with its capacious appetite for news, and with the press's easily generated outrage at being kept away from what is happening, the secrecy rule in 1787 would not be viable. But the secrecy rule gave the Convention a shield for its candor. In no other setting could such a document have been built. On the motion of Pierce Butler of South Carolina, the Convention voted "that no copy be taken of any entry on the journal during the sitting of the house without leave of the house. That members only be permitted to inspect the journal. That nothing spoken in the house be printed or otherwise published or communicated without leave."

The sheer audacity of the rule is brazen, even in those times. Today, it is quite possible that television trucks, armed newsmen, and hordes of commentators clutching large microphones would attack any house declaring that rule, showering invective and editorial mace on all who resisted. It is also quite possible that no man who voted for the secrecy rule would dare be interviewed again.

The invoking of the secrecy rule in many ways is not as spectacular as the respecting of it. In this loose-tongued, garrulous group, there were no suspensions from the rule. Madison, who told of the secrecy to his cousin, the president of William and Mary, got this tart reply back from his inquisitive relative: "If you cannot tell us what you are doing, you might at least give us some information of what you are *not* doing." Few newspapers seemed to want to engage the Convention in a quarrel about the rule, and few made visible their irritation. Again, it was Jefferson who was still the rebel. He wrote John Adams that the "precedent of tying up the tongues of the delegates was abominable."

Antidemocratic, yes, the secrecy rule surely was. But it has been pointed out by many historians that it was two antidemocratic resolves which were necessary to give the Constitution a chance to be born. One was the certainly undemocratic method of selecting delegates so that the petulant and the disaffected were omitted from those sent to Philadelphia; the second was the secrecy invocation.

In later years, Madison frankly admitted that no Constitution would have been brought forth, nor adopted, if the debates had been made public.

The second safeguard was the utilization of the Committee of the Whole House. This was an aged parliamentary device invented by the House of Commons in order to give its members freedom from the long and debasing arm of a tyrant ruler. In the Commons the mace, symbol of royal authority, would be put out of sight; so long as it remained out of sight, votes were not recorded but were test votes, so that the House could see how the debate was breaking and judge the direction final decisions would take.

Whenever the Convention went into the Committee of the Whole, the most ticklish and thorny problems would be debated, votes taken, with every member secure in the knowledge that when the Convention reconvened from under the Committee of the Whole, after the fullest and frankest kind of debate, final voting could be recorded with some certainty that what was finally done was right. This allowing of votes to be taken without the tight binding of finality, given as it were without pledge or endorsement, made the Committee of the Whole a continually useful device to lubricate the debates, and ventilate both the stubborn and the certain.

There would be little to report of an intimate or even accurate nature if James Madison had not been diligent beyond normal limits. He took notes, copious notes, full and ready notes, each day. He was both the unofficial secretary of the Convention, as well as its goad and prime architect. He knew then that posterity—the men of the Convention were quite able to understand that posterity would long note and seriously remember what they did—would embrace these precious notes with hospitable interest. He himself reports:

> I chose a seat in front of the presiding member, with the other members on my right and left hand. In this favorable position for hearing all that passed, I noted . . . what was read from the chair or spoken by members; and losing not a moment unnecessarily between the adjournment and re-assembling of the Convention, I was enabled to write out my daily notes during the session or within a few finishing days after its close. In the labor and correctness of this I was not a little aided by practice,

> and by a familiarity with the style and train of observation and reasoning which characterized the principal speakers. It happened also that I was not absent a single day, nor more than a casual fraction of an hour in any day, so that I could not have lost a single speech, unless a very short one.

This prodigious assignment, voluntarily assumed, is a treasure trove for the historian and the interested reader. This application of diligence and discipline is typical of Madison, who, alone among the delegates, arrived days early and began his final readjustment of his notes, ideas, and plans, most of which Governor Edmund Randolph presented early in the Convention under the description "the Virginia Plan." In truth, as most historians record, it was Randolph's voice, Virginia's choice, but Madison's work.

A curious by-piece of history is how and when Madison's notes became public. He resisted all efforts to pry the notes from him during his life. Not more than a handful of close friends even knew of their existence. The honoring of the secrecy rule among the delegates *after* the Convention seems incredible in our own age of instant "kiss-and-tell," wherein public servants are reading their books in galley proofs almost before the ink is dry on their resignations from office. Not until 1836, when Madison died at age eighty-six, nearly fifty years after the signing of the Constitution, did his will indicate that his notes were ready for publication. (Congress paid his wife a substantial sum for the rights, and in 1840 the "Notes of Madison" were finally opened to the public.)

There were other note takers, including the official secretary of the Convention, Major Jackson. Others were William Pierce (whose summations of his colleagues' character and physical presence are colorful and unique, though not completely accurate), Robert Yates of New York, Hamilton, James McHenry of Maryland, and Rufus King of Massachusetts. These were the eyewitness reporters. All others must record their histories from what some participant said (memory is a tricky compound and vanity an unreliable alloy), or they must take their facts from those who were there and whose observations were at least more warmly resident in the actual moment.

The delegates met at the State House in Philadelphia. In this building the Continental Congress had done its business, and in this place had been signed the Declaration of Independence.

The room in which they met was large, and though it had a cool look about it, the Philadelphia air during the '87 summer hung moist and still too often for comfort. The windows were tall and wide, and through their gracious openings the light, spangled and bright, invaded the meeting. The ceilings were high, giving the great room a grace confirmed by the delicate moldings over the arched doorways and girdling the walls. Delegates sat at tables, three or four to a table, with their notes and papers on the green baize that covered the old wood. Their work schedule was disciplined, and for this kind of conclave, rigorous. They set an agenda of five-hour days, six days a week. This left time for private conferences, speech writing, preparation of ideas, correspondence, and the lobbying that never slackened. Decorum all through the long hot summer never lost its shape, and though the debate became furious at times, and though some of the delegates (like Luther Martin) ranted and shouted for what must have seemed like unendurable eternities, there was never an evidence of tempers fraying to the snapping point, or violence becoming visible. There was in this proceeding a never-to-be-breached coverlet of civilized, intelligent controversy.

And so the Convention began its work.

Almost immediately, Governor Randolph presented the Virginia Plan, which in many ways resembled the final Constitution. This was the labored intellectual handiwork of Madison, and it set forth the strong national government so much admired by him and Hamilton and a goodly number of others who reckoned liberty as the cohabitor of the land with order, and who believed that order could emerge only from a national instrument with both the power and the resolve to act when necessary.

With the presentation of the Virginia Plan, the first significant confrontation began, the bloody battle between the small states and the large states. At issue: How to elect the Congress.

From mid-June on, the jousting between the opposing factions bracketed every thought and speech of the delegates.

The war between the large-state men, who wanted proportional representation, and the small-state men, who demanded equal representation, had begun. It was to be both relentless and rancorous, steadily exhausting and dividing the delegates until sensible compromise could be effected.

George Read of Delaware set the stage when he announced that Delaware would withdraw from the Convention if proportional representation won the day. Thereupon the delegates tackled the least poisonous of senatorial issues, who would select senators?

Roger Sherman frowned on the people making this choice, or indeed selecting anyone for public office. "The people should have little to do with government, for they are apt to be misled," was Sherman's view.

Elbridge Gerry of Massachusetts endorsed Sherman. But George Mason of Virginia and James Wilson of Pennsylvania moved to head off what they considered as a rush to aristocracy. Wilson compared the government to be created to a pyramid, insisting that its endurance depended on a broad base. "It is on the people that the government must rest," he said, and Wilson's homely metaphor illuminated the direction of the prodemocrats in the meeting. (Throughout the debates, Wilson's calm, thrusting, precise arguments never slackened in his pursuit of direct election by the people for both Congress and the chief executive. It was his suggestion on June 2 for states to be divided into districts and qualified voters to select electors who would name the president. This was the seedbed of the electoral college, a bitter concession by stubborn delegates insisting on state legislatures as the selectors of the president.)

When, on June 6, Gerry paraded the Massachusetts legislature as Exhibit A to illustrate how low in esteem and ability a popularly elected body could depress itself, Wilson quickly answered that the only legitimate authority was the people and "the legislature should be the exact transcript of the people."

Finally, John Dickinson's motion to have the Senate elected by state legislatures overpowered Wilson and his like-minded colleagues, and the Convention so voted—a rule to stand until the Seventeenth Amendment, affirmed May 31, 1913, which at last vindicated the Wilson idea and ideal.

Now, the great fragile strand of unity stretched to its snapping point, and along this sheer, tightly drawn thread, the debaters walked so warily and dangerously: small states versus large states colliding over the chasm on the issue of how to people the Senate, equally or proportionally?

Paterson of New Jersey hurled the meeting into disarray when he angrily urged the small states to depart before they were swallowed up.

Madison rebutted Paterson. How dare fifty New Jerseymen outweigh one hundred and fifty Pennsylvanians, demanded Madison. There was no justice in this, and moreover, continued Madison, unless the states were not willing to part with sovereignty, it was folly to talk of government.

The heat and the hackles rose. The meeting neared a breaking edge, and adjournment until the next day saved further torment and possible disaster.

June 11 was the crucial day. Connecticut's Roger Sherman offered a resolution, destined to lose at that time, but designed, though he did not know it, to be the great compromise of the Convention and the linchpin to which every other decision connected, and without which it is fair to declare that the Convention would have been so sorely crippled that it could not have done its business.

The Sherman resolution was to propose that the proportion of voting in the House of Representatives (called the "First Branch" by Sherman) should be according to the respective numbers of free inhabitants; and that in the second branch, or Senate, each state should have one vote and no more.

This was it, the profoundest resolution of the entire meeting. It was not to be decided finally on June 11; there would be rages, and logic and cajolements and threats yet to be made. "When a great question is first started," said John Adams, "there are very few, even of the greatest minds, which suddenly and instinctively comprehend it in all its consequences."

The unsettling fact of the debate is the unyielding opposition of Madison. This sensitive and intuitive man, so aware, almost tactile in his understanding of the subtleties of politics—that he should be the irreconcilable foe of the compromise is a puzzling indictment of Madison. The great compromise was the only pragmatic alternative, and to a man like Madison, so attached to the federal system, the idea of balance, of putting the scales level, ought to have had splendid attraction, so much did it resemble his own inventive turn of mind.

On June 11, the vote was against Sherman and his compromise, mainly because the arithmetic of "how" the population was to be counted could not be resolved. But the good sense of this alternative remained alive and would be considered again.

The ultimate solution came in typical Convention fashion: a committee was appointed to sort out the arguments and come up with a compromise. In the composition of the committee was the herald of Wilson's and Madison's defeat, for those chosen were by far leaners to the cause of the compromise: Gerry, Ellsworth, Paterson, Franklin, Bedford, Martin, Davie, Baldwin, Mason, and Rutledge.

This resort to committee, insulated from wrangling and invective no matter how stylishly phrased, was, time and again, a ploy of strength and prudence, and it always worked.

The committee reported back on July 2. The initial suggestion by Sherman had been given sufficiency and root by the committee, and again the instinctive pragmatism of the delegates was visible. In order to placate the equal representation men, the right of origination of all bills for raising or appropriating money was given to the first house.

Wilson stormily denounced the committee report, but his support slipped away, even though a decisive vote was avoided at the time.

With as much of the bitterness as possible extracted, on July 16 the delegates took the most valuable vote in the Convention, and established once and for all the vital distribution of the Congress—proportional representation in the House, equal vote in the Senate. The tally on July 19 was five states (Connecticut, New Jersey, Delaware, Maryland, North Carolina) *for,* and four states (Pennsylvania, Virginia, South Carolina, Georgia) *against.*

But on June 11, there also began the resolution of the second of the unsolvable problems, how to adjust the arithmetic of counting population, and thus, how to count slaves in the proportional representation. Congress in 1783 had already created the so-called "three-fifths" rule, whereby five slaves would be counted equal to three free men. A precedent had already been erected. Now it was to be picked up and examined once more.

Before Sherman's suggestion could take final form, it was quite obvious that the question of how to count the people (which would in turn determine how many representatives would enter the House) must be decided.

The sneers and the bitterness of the northerners filled the hall. "Blacks are property," said Gerry, "and used to the southward as horses and cattle to the northward. Why then should not horses and cattle have the right of representation in the north?"

The nation would not hear the last of this, but the Convention could not stall. James Wilson moved that the three-fifths rule be adopted. This rule intruded into the Constitution and was to be the law of the land until the Fourteenth Amendment in 1868.

The final settling of the slavery question came in August, in the waning days of the Convention. The three-fifths rule stood, and in return the southern states agreed that the importation of slaves would come to an end in 1808.

There was much haggling, some backing and filling, and much denouncing, outrage, invective, and counter-diatribe. Gouverneur Morris poured out an envenomed picture of a south made miserable and barren by slavery. Roger Sherman thought slavery "iniquitous," but chose not to oppose it. Mason blamed the British for stoking the slave trade, and indicted the New Englanders for lusting after slave-trade dollars even as they professed to be abolitionists. The response from the New Englanders was icy, to say the least; moralists discomfort very easily. The southerners were happily silent during this exchange.

But it was finally done. One of the biggest of the crucial, explosive issues had been hammered away. Hamilton thought that without the federal ratio no union could have been formed. The issue was central to the unification of the new nation.

The third great question of the Convention, the one on which so much hinged and about which more votes were taken, and more debate produced and more plans set forth than any other thorny question, was the problem of the chief executive, or, as the Virginia Plan had put it, in its Resolve Number 7: ". . . that a national executive be instituted." No mention of number or form, only a national executive, and from this early declaration came the hottest, most querulous, and most thoughtful of all dialogue within the meeting.

The Virginia Plan envisioned an executive to be elected by the legislature, protected in compensation, ineligible for re-election, and possessor of a "general authority" to enforce the laws of the land.

The Committee of the Whole reported back to the Convention

on June 13 with a set of nineteen resolutions, mainly fitted and shaped to the Virginia Plan. This report called for a single executive with a seven-year term, chosen by the legislature, still ineligible for re-election, and who could be removed if he were impeached and convicted of "malpractices or neglect of duty."

The first discussion of the executive began when the Convention dutifully formed into a Committee of the Whole. No one in these early debates called the position "president." It was to be some time before this label attached itself to the post; indeed, there was some lag before James Wilson rose to move a "single executive." There was in that Convention a touch of terror in the cataloguing of a single person as head of the government. This was boggy ground, for it smacked of monarchy, a despot despoiling all that had been so fiercely fought for and won. Though the states had a single executive, the legislatures commanded all the power and had absolute control over the governor or the president of the state.

Here it was Wilson again, with his clear, penetrating legal mind, who gave sustenance to the logic of the single man as chief. His carefully structured thoughts marched in serried ranks through all this discussion, armed with tailored logic, impervious to anything except logic-in-kind. He inveighed against a plural executive and cited the sorry examples of Athens and the Decemvirs of Rome. Energy, dispatch, and responsibility were the key assets to be resident in a chief executive. Wilson's assessments proved to be the most prescient of all the delegates. With unerring aim, he hit exactly the prime necessities in a president.

George Mason and Edmund Randolph protested the single source, and argued for a plural executive. There was much pull and tug over historical precedents, and the specter of despots rose mistily from the floor a dozen times, brandished like some ghostly wand by those who feared the power of a vigorous, determined single executive.

The Whig influence, never really too far beneath the surface of debate, clung to suspicions and doubts about a single chief executive.

How to elect the president was a snake pit of confusion and wild surmise, ranging from election by electors chosen by the state legislatures to election by state governors or by electors chosen by them; nomination by the people of each state of "its best citizen," and election from this reservoir of best men by the national legislature; election by the national legislature with electors chosen by the state legislatures taking over whenever an executive sought re-election; election by a small group of national legislators chosen by lot; and, the most bizarre proposal of them all (initiated by Wilson and Gouverneur Morris), that the executive be elected directly by the people. The latter suggestion was deemed so ridiculous, even dangerous, that only Pennsylvania voted for it.

On August 31, the presidential matter was still unresolved, a bone in the throat of the delegates and one they determined to extract. A Committee on Postponed Matters was proposed and organized. It was the duty of this group to assemble all the arguments about all the issues still not settled, put them into proposals, and bring them back to the meeting. It was, as one historian put it, a rescue party to make up the Convention's mind.

From this Committee came the first of several presidential specifications. He was to be thirty-five, at least fourteen years resident in the country, and either a natural-born citizen or a citizen of the United States at the time of the adoption of the Constitution. But the significant thrust of the Committee's work was the method of selecting the president. By now, they had settled on a four-year term (it was no occult measure or specifically logical length of time; more probably it was the least offensive of a number of suggestions), with eligibility for re-election (Benjamin Franklin was the strongest influence for re-election of the president). The key element was a system for election of electors from each state, with the state to determine how the electors were to be chosen, equal in number to the representatives from that state in the Congress. These electors would meet at home and vote by ballot for two persons, of whom one could not be an inhabitant from the state. Remember, the delegates were practical men, and they assumed that the electors would naturally vote for men from their own state. Moreover, the votes were to be counted by the Senate, and the man having the greatest number of votes, providing it was a majority of the electors, would be president. If no man had a majority, the Senate would choose the chief executive from the top five. The man with the second highest number of votes would be vice president.

But the fear of senatorial encroachments, this fear of great lords of power occupying the second branch, still pervaded the delegates. Thus, it was they (led by Wilson, Dickinson, Sherman, Madison, Williamson, and Mason) who stripped the Senate of this arbitrary persuasion and passed it to the House, with each state delegation having but one vote. Both large and small-state men bought this plan, and it was written into the Constitution by a ten-to-one vote of the Convention.

When the Committee on Postponed Matters had finished its task, and the Convention had re-patterned and re-formed, the cast of the president's office and power was nearly complete. He had a fixed term and compensation; he was the administrative head of the government, with a source of power in his election separated if not divorced from the Congress; he was apparently going to be a unique being in that he would be head of the government as well as ceremonial chief of state. He held a qualified veto over the Congress's activities, and he could convene them on extraordinary occasions. He had developed into a vital and sturdy figure, in whose person and office resided dignity and the possibility of strength.

And yet, even as the delegates labored over the blueprint of the presidency, there was no doubt in anyone's mind as to whom the mantle of this power would surely fall. General Washington, without raising his voice or involving himself in the debates, without any pretense of authority or sign of impatience, was the certain choice to be the first president. Benjamin Franklin, on June 4, predicted that the "first man put at the helm will be a good one." He did not attempt to spell out to whom he was referring. The entire assemblage knew. The most unreconstructed Whig among the delegates was comforted by the notion that the General would be the first chief executive, and could be elected again and again until he either died or chose not to seek re-election. When the delegates surveyed their work and possibly may have determined that they had constructed a really awesome figure of a president, they probably would have responded as did Pierce Butler when he wrote a relative about the vast accumulation of authority in the leader of the nation: . . . "nor do I believe they would have been so great [referring to the large presidential powers] had not many of the members cast their eyes towards General Washington as President; and shaped their ideas of the powers to be given a President, by their opinions of his virtues."

The first jokes about the vice president had their origins when Williamson, rather dryly, remarked that the vice presidency was an anomalous office introduced only for the sake of an election that required two to be chosen at the same time.

But the mosaic was now fully in place. The presidency was set and formed and fixed. There were still some diehards. Gouverneur Morris, Hamilton, and Read grumbled for their theory of tenure for life, and still advocated an absolute veto on the part of the president. Wilson, Read, Carroll, and Morris reluctantly went along with the election mode; they still declared in favor of a direct election by the people. James Wilson lamented that the president could become the minion of the Senate (again Wilson's clairvoyance sharpens with age, as in this last third of the twentieth century, the Senate once more defies the president in his reach for power in the foreign policy field, and bids him retract the directives exercised by earlier presidents).

Madison demanded that the Supreme Court have a share in the presidential veto, which, he claimed, would put steel in the spine of a weak president under attack by a ferocious Congress. Gouverneur Morris favored the chief justice as the first in line to succeed a dead president. Martin and Gerry wanted to fix the size of the army. Charles Pinckney urged a property qualification high enough to bar any presidential candidate except the very rich like himself. Williamson and Mason wanted three chief executives instead of one.

It was Rossiter's view that the president emerged from the debates more splendidly equipped with what he needed to establish his pre-eminence than even the wildest dreamer of presidential power could have hoped. It is a bit tingling to remember that, two weeks before the end of the Convention, the Senate still held exclusive authority to appoint ambassadors and judges and to make treaties. How cheerless it is to contemplate, muses Rossiter, that a few really stubborn men in Philadelphia, had they stuck to their course, could have won election of the president by the legislature.

The large, essential work was done.

Monday afternoon at four o'clock on September 17, 1787, the Convention adjourned, and the work of ratification began.

The language of the Constitution, mostly the work of Gouverneur Morris, was plain and clear. There were no ornate flourishes, no baroque soundings of theme and cause; there was only the scouring sweep of the clauses each fitted squarely into place.

The creation of the men at Philadelphia has weathered storm and controversy, the dirty clash of families and brothers, the clawing and the jawing of demagogues and traitors, as well as the well-meaning incursions of petty patriots and blind, stupid blunderers.

No one of the framers would have described what he shared in as a perfect conjunction of harmony and intellect. There was in each of the delegates a sense of the absent, some piece that was unfinished, some part that was undone, some portion that was left out. But all would have agreed with Franklin that it was the best that could have been achieved, and on that measure alone he was willing to be counted a supporter. By whatever delicate calipers one uses, it cannot be disputed that this Constitution, garmented to fit four million people in a restless moment of insurrection and rebirth, has lasted almost two hundred years, and has expanded and enlarged without fracturing or shattering to suit the ambitions and the needs of two hundred million citizens. This is the surprise and wonder of it all, and if one is perplexed by how it happened, one must also be cheered by the fact that it did happen.

Alfred North Whitehead paid the Constitution its ultimate tribute when he wrote: "The men who founded your republic had an uncommonly clear grasp of the general ideas that they wanted to put in here, then left the working out of the details to later interpreters, which has been, on the whole, remarkably successful. I know of only three times in the Western World when statesmen consciously took control of historic destinies: Periclean Athens, Rome under Augustus and the founding of your American republic."

To get the full flavor of the Constitutional Convention in all its splendid drama, I suggest two books. They are immensely readable, historically accurate, and once picked up are hard to put down: *1787—The Grand Convention* by Clinton Rossiter, and *Miracle at Philadelphia* by Catherine Drinker Bowen.

CONSTITUTION OF THE UNITED STATES OF AMERICA

We the People of the United States, in Order to form a more perfect Union, establish Justice, insure domestic Tranquility, provide for the common defence, promote the general Welfare, and secure the Blessings of Liberty to ourselves and our Posterity, do ordain and establish this CONSTITUTION for the United States of America.

Article I

Section 1. All legislative Powers herein granted shall be vested in a Congress of the United States, which shall consist of a Senate and House of Representatives.

Section 2. The House of Representatives shall be composed of Members chosen every second Year by the People of the several States, and the Electors in each State shall have the Qualifications requisite for Electors of the most numerous Branch of the State Legislature.

No Person shall be a Representative who shall not have attained to the Age of twenty-five Years, and been seven Years a Citizen of the United States, and who shall not when elected, be an Inhabitant of that State in which he shall be chosen.

Representatives and direct Taxes shall be apportioned among the several States which may be included within this Union according to their respective Numbers, which shall be determined by adding to the whole Number of free Persons, including those bound to Service for a Term of Years, and excluding Indians not taxed, three fifths of all other Persons. The actual Enumeration shall be made within three Years after the first Meeting of the Congress of the United States, and within every subsequent Term of ten Years, in such Manner as they shall by Law direct. The Number of Representatives shall not exceed one for every thirty Thousand, but each State shall have at Least one Representative; and until such enumeration shall be made, the State of New Hampshire shall be entitled to chuse three, Massachusetts eight, Rhode-Island and Providence Plantations one, Connecticut five, New-York six, New Jersey four, Pennsylvania eight, Delaware one, Maryland six, Virginia ten, North Carolina five, South Carolina five, and Georgia three.

When vacancies happen in the Representation from any State, the Executive Authority thereof shall issue Writs of Election to fill such Vacancies.

The House of Representatives shall chuse their Speaker and other Officers; and shall have the sole Power of Impeachment.

Section 3. The Senate of the United States shall be composed of two Senators from each State, chosen by the Legislature thereof, for six Years; and each Senator shall have one Vote.

Immediately after they shall be assembled in Consequence of the first Election, they shall be divided as equally as may be into three Classes. The Seats of the Senators of the first Class shall be vacated at the Expiration of the Second Year, of the second Class at the Expiration of the fourth Year, and of the third Class at the Expiration of the sixth Year, so that one-third may be chosen every second Year; and if Vacancies happen by Resignation, or otherwise, during the Recess of the Legislature of any State, the Executive thereof may make temporary Appointments until the next Meeting of the Legislature, which shall then fill such Vacancies.

No Person shall be a Senator who shall not have attained to the Age of thirty Years, and been nine Years a Citizen of the United States, and who shall not, when elected, be an Inhabitant of that State for which he shall be chosen.

The Vice President of the United States shall be President of the Senate, but shall have no Vote, unless they be equally divided.

The Senate shall chuse their other Officers, and also a President pro tempore, in the absence of the Vice President, or when he shall exercise the Office of President of the United States.

The Senate shall have the sole Power to try all Impeachments. When sitting for that Purpose, they shall be on Oath or Affirmation. When the President of the United States is tried, the Chief Justice shall preside: And no Person shall be convicted without the Concurrence of two-thirds of the Members present.

Judgment in Cases of Impeachment shall not extend further than to removal from Office, and disqualification to hold and enjoy any Office of honor, Trust, or Profit under the United States; but the Party convicted shall nevertheless be liable and subject to Indictment, Trial, Judgment, and Punishment, according to Law.

Section 4. The Times, Places and Manner of holding Elections for Senators and Representatives, shall be prescribed in each State by the Legislature thereof; but the Congress may at any time by Law make or alter such Regulations, except as to the Places of chusing Senators.

The Congress shall assemble at least once in every Year, and such Meeting shall be on the first Monday in December, unless they shall by Law appoint a different Day.

Section 5. Each House shall be the Judge of the Elections, Returns, and Qualifications of its own Members, and a Majority of each shall constitute a Quorum to do Business; but a smaller Number may adjourn from day to day, and may be authorized to compel the Attendance of absent Members, in such Manner, and under such Penalties as Each House may provide.

Each House may determine the Rules of its Proceedings, punish its Members for disorderly Behavior, and, with the Concurrence of two thirds, expel a Member.

Each House shall keep a Journal of its Proceedings, and from time to time publish the same, excepting such Parts as may in their Judgment require Secrecy; and the Yeas and Nays of the Members of either House on any question shall, at the Desire of one fifth of those Present, be entered on the Journal.

Neither House, during the Session of Congress, shall, without the Consent of the other, adjourn for more than three days, nor to any other Place than that in which the two Houses shall be sitting.

Section 6. The Senators and Representatives shall receive a Compensation for their Services, to be ascertained by Law, and paid out of the Treasury of the United States. They shall in all Cases, except Treason, Felony and Breach of the Peace, be privileged from Arrest during their Attendance at the Session of their respective Houses, and in going to and returning from the same; and for any Speech or Debate in either House, they shall not be questioned in any other Place.

No Senator or Representative shall, during the Time for which he was elected, be appointed to any civil Office under the Authority of the United States, which shall have been created, or the Emoluments whereof shall have been encreased during such time; and no Person holding any Office under the United States, shall be a Member of either House during his Continuance in Office.

Section 7. All Bills for raising Revenue shall originate in the House of Representatives; but the Senate may propose or concur with Amendments as on other Bills.

Every Bill which shall have passed the House of Representatives and the Senate, shall, before it become a Law, be presented to the President of the United States; if he approve he shall sign it, but if not he shall return it, with his Objections to that House in which it shall have originated, who shall enter the Objections at large on their Journal, and proceed to reconsider it. If after such Reconsideration two thirds of that House shall agree to pass the Bill, it shall be sent, together with the Objections, to the other House, by which it shall likewise be reconsidered, and if approved by two thirds of that House, it shall become a Law. But in all such Cases the Votes of both Houses shall be determined by Yeas and Nays, and the Names of the Persons voting for and against the Bill shall be entered on the Journal of each House respectively. If any Bill shall not be returned by the President within ten Days (Sundays excepted) after it shall have been presented to him, the Same shall be a Law, in like Manner as if he had signed it, unless the Congress by their Adjournment prevent its Return, in which Case it shall not be a Law.

Every Order, Resolution, or Vote to which the Concurrence of the Senate and House of Representatives may be necessary (except on a question of Adjournment) shall be presented to the President of the United States; and before the Same shall take Effect, shall be approved by him, or being disapproved by him, shall be repassed by two thirds of the Senate and House of Representatives, according to the Rules and Limitations prescribed in the Case of a Bill.

Section 8. The Congress shall have Power To lay and collect Taxes, Duties, Imposts and Excises, to pay the Debts and provide for the common Defense and general Welfare of the

United States; but all Duties, Imposts and Excises shall be uniform throughout the United States;

To borrow money on the credit of the United States;

To regulate Commerce with foreign Nations, and among the several states, and with the Indian Tribes;

To establish an uniform Rule of Naturalization, and uniform Laws on the subject of Bankruptcies throughout the United States;

To coin Money, regulate the Value thereof, and of foreign Coin, and fix the Standard of Weights and Measures;

To provide for the Punishment of counterfeiting the Securities and current Coin of the United States;

To establish Post Offices and post Roads;

To promote the Progress of Science and useful Arts, by securing for limited Times to Authors and Inventors the exclusive Rights to their respective Writings and Discoveries;

To constitute Tribunals inferior to the supreme Court;

To define and punish Piracies and Felonies committed on the high Seas, and Offenses against the Law of Nations;

To declare War, grant Letters of Marque and Reprisal, and make Rules concerning Captures on Land and Water;

To raise and support Armies, but no Appropriation of Money to that Use shall be for a longer Term than two Years;

To provide and maintain a Navy;

To make Rules for the Government and Regulation of the land and naval Forces;

To provide for calling forth the Militia to execute the Laws of the Union, suppress Insurrections and repel Invasions;

To provide for organizing, arming, and disciplining the Militia, and for governing such Part of them as may be employed in the Service of the United States, reserving to the States respectively, the Appointment of the Officers, and the Authority of training the Militia according to the discipline prescribed by Congress;

To exercise exclusive Legislation in all Cases whatsoever,

over such District (not exceeding ten Miles square) as may, by Cession of particular States, and the acceptance of Congress, become the Seat of the Government of the United States, and to exercise like Authority over all Places purchased by the Consent of the Legislature of the State in which the Same shall be, for the Erection of Forts, Magazines, Arsenals, dock-Yards, and other needful Buildings;—And

To make all Laws which shall be necessary and proper for carrying into Execution the foregoing Powers, and all other Powers vested by this Constitution in the Government of the United States, or in any Department or Officer thereof.

Section 9. The Migration or Importation of Such Persons as any of the States now existing shall think proper to admit, shall not be prohibited by the Congress prior to the Year one thousand eight hundred and eight, but a tax or duty may be imposed on such Importation, not exceeding ten dollars for each Person.

The privilege of the Writ of Habeas Corpus shall not be suspended, unless when in Cases of Rebellion or Invasion the Public Safety may require it.

No Bill of Attainder or ex post facto Law shall be passed.

No capitation, or other direct, Tax shall be laid, unless in Proportion to the Census or Enumeration herein before directed to be taken.

No Tax or Duty shall be laid on Articles exported from any State.

No preference shall be given by any Regulation of Commerce or Revenue to the Ports of one State over those of another: nor shall Vessels bound to, or from, one State be obliged to enter, clear, or pay Duties in another.

No Money shall be drawn from the Treasury, but in Consequence of Appropriations made by Law; and a regular Statement and Account of the Receipts and Expenditures of all public Money shall be published from time to time.

No Title of Nobility shall be granted by the United States: And no Person holding any Office of Profit or Trust under them, shall, without the Consent of the Congress, accept of any present, Emolument, Office, or Title, of any kind whatever, from any King, Prince, or foreign State.

Section 10. No State shall enter into any Treaty, Alliance, or Confederation; grant Letters of Marque and Reprisal; coin Money; emit Bills of Credit; make any Thing but gold and silver Coin a Tender in Payment of Debts; pass any Bill of Attainder, ex post facto Law, or Law impairing the Obligation of Contracts, or grant any Title of Nobility.

No State shall, without the Consent of the Congress, lay any Imposts or Duties on Imports or Exports, except what may be absolutely necessary for executing its inspection Laws; and the net Produce of all Duties and Imposts, laid by any State on Imports or Exports, shall be for the Use of the Treasury of the United States; and all such Laws shall be subject to the Revision and Control of the Congress.

No State shall, without the Consent of Congress, lay any duty of Tonnage, keep Troops, or Ships of War in time of Peace, enter into any Agreement or Compact with another State, or with a foreign Power, or engage in War, unless actually invaded, or in such imminent Danger as will not admit of delay.

Article ii

Section 1. The executive Power shall be vested in a President of the United States of America. He shall hold his Office during the Term of four Years, and, together with the Vice-President, chosen for the same Term, be elected, as follows:

Each State shall appoint, in such Manner as the Legislature thereof may direct, a Number of Electors, equal to the whole Number of Senators and Representatives to which the State may be entitled in the Congress: but no Senator or Representative, or Person holding an Office of Trust or Profit under the United States, shall be appointed an Elector.

The Electors shall meet in their respective States, and vote by Ballot for two persons, of whom one at least shall not be an Inhabitant of the same State with themselves. And they shall make a List of all the Persons voted for, and of the Number of Votes for each; which List they shall sign and certify, and transmit sealed to the Seat of the Government of the United States, directed to the President of the Senate. The President of the Senate shall, in the Presence of the Senate and House of Representatives, open all the Certificates, and the Votes shall then be counted. The Person having the greatest Number of Votes shall be the President, if such Number be a Majority of the whole Number of Electors appointed; and if there be more than one who have such Majority, and have an equal Number of Votes, then the House of Representatives shall immediately chuse by Ballot one of them for President; and if no Person have a Majority, then from the five highest on the List the said House shall in like Manner chuse the President. But in chusing the President, the Votes shall be taken by States, the Representation from each State having one Vote; A quorum for this Purpose shall consist of a Member or Members from two-thirds of the States, and a Majority of all the States shall be necessary to a Choice. In every Case, after the Choice of the President, the Person having the greatest Number of Votes of the Electors shall be the Vice President. But if there should remain two or more who have equal Votes, the Senate shall chuse from them by Ballot the Vice-President.

The Congress may determine the Time of chusing the Electors, and the Day on which they shall give their Votes; which Day shall be the same throughout the United States.

No Person except a natural born Citizen, or a Citizen of the United States, at the time of the Adoption of this Constitution, shall be eligible to the Office of President; neither shall any Person be eligible to that Office who shall not have attained to the Age of thirty-five Years, and been fourteen Years a Resident within the United States.

In case of the Removal of the President from Office, or of his Death, Resignation, or Inability to discharge the Powers and Duties of the said Office, the same shall devolve on the Vice President, and the Congress may by Law provide for the Case of Removal, Death, Resignation or Inability, both of the President and Vice President, declaring what Officer shall then act as President, and such Officer shall act accordingly, until the Disability be removed, or a President shall be elected.

The President shall, at stated Times, receive for his Services, a Compensation, which shall neither be encreased nor diminished during the Period for which he shall have been elected, and he shall not receive within the Period any other Emolument from the United States, or any of them.

Before he enter on the Execution of his Office, he shall take the following Oath or Affirmation:—"I do solemnly swear (or affirm) that I will faithfully execute the Office of President of the United States, and will to the best of my Ability, preserve, protect and defend the Constitution of the United States."

Section 2. The President shall be Commander in Chief of the Army and Navy of the United States, and of the Militia of the several States, when called into the actual Service of the United States; he may require the Opinion, in writing, of the principal Officer in each of the executive Departments, upon any subject relating to the Duties of their respective Offices, and he shall have Power to grant Reprieves and Pardons for Offenses against the United States, except in Cases of Impeachment.

He shall have Power, by and with the Advice and Consent of the Senate, to make Treaties, provided two-thirds of the

Senators present concur; and he shall nominate, and by and with the Advice and Consent of the Senate, shall appoint Ambassadors, other public Ministers and Consuls, Judges of the supreme Court, and all other Officers of the United States, whose Appointments are not herein otherwise provided for, and which shall be established by Law; but the Congress may by Law vest the Appointment of such inferior Officers, as they think proper, in the President alone, in the Courts of Law, or in the Heads of Departments.

The President shall have Power to fill up all Vacancies that may happen during the Recess of the Senate, by granting Commissions which shall expire at the End of their next Session.

Section 3. He shall from time to time give to the Congress Information of the State of the Union, and recommend to their Consideration such Measures as he shall judge necessary and expedient; he may, on extraordinary Occasions, convene both Houses, or either of them, and in Case of Disagreement between them, with Respect to the Time of Adjournment, he may adjourn them to such Time as he shall think proper; he shall receive Ambassadors and other public Ministers; he shall take Care that the Laws be faithfully executed, and shall Commission all the Officers of the United States.

Section 4. The President, Vice President and all civil Officers of the United States, shall be removed from Office on Impeachment for, and Conviction of, Treason, Bribery, or other high Crimes and Misdemeanors.

Article iii

Section 1. The judicial Power of the United States, shall be vested in one supreme Court, and in such inferior Courts as the Congress may from time to time ordain and establish. The

Judges, both of the supreme and inferior Courts, shall hold their offices during good Behavior, and shall, at stated Times, receive for their Services a Compensation which shall not be diminished during their Continuance in Office.

Section 2. The judicial Power shall extend to all Cases, in Law and Equity, arising under this Constitution, the Laws of the United States, and Treaties made, or which shall be made, under their Authority;—to all Cases affecting Ambassadors, other public Ministers and Consuls;—to all Cases of admiralty and maritime Jurisdiction;—to Controversies to which the United States shall be a Party;—to Controversies between two or more States;—between a State and Citizens of another State;—between Citizens of different States;—between Citizens of the same State claiming Lands under Grants of different States, and between a State, or the Citizens thereof, and foreign States, Citizens or Subjects.

In all Cases affecting Ambassadors, other public Ministers and Consuls, and those in which a State shall be a Party, the supreme Court shall have original Jurisdiction. In all the other Cases before mentioned, the supreme Court shall have appellate Jurisdiction, both as to Law and Fact, with such Exceptions, and under such Regulations as the Congress shall make.

The trial of all Crimes, except in Cases of Impeachment, shall be by Jury; and such Trial shall be held in the State where the said Crimes shall have been committed; but when not committed within any State, the Trial shall be at such Place or Places as the Congress may by Law have directed.

Section 3. Treason against the United States, shall consist only in levying War against them, or, in adhering to their Enemies, giving them Aid and Comfort. No Person shall be convicted of Treason unless on the Testimony of two Witnesses to the same overt Act, or on Confession in open Court.

The Congress shall have power to declare the Punishment of Treason, but no Attainder of Treason shall work Corruption of Blood, or Forfeiture except during the Life of the Person attained.

Article iv

Section 1. Full Faith and Credit shall be given in each State to the public Acts, Records, and judicial Proceedings of every other State. And the Congress may by general Laws prescribe the Manner in which such Acts, Records and Proceedings shall be proved, and the Effect thereof.

Section 2. The Citizens of each State shall be entitled to all Privileges and Immunities of Citizens in the several States.

A Person charged in any State with Treason, Felony, or other Crime, who shall flee from Justice, and be found in another State, shall on demand of the executive Authority of the State from which he fled, be delivered up, to be removed to the State having Jurisdiction of the Crime.

No Person held to Service or Labour in one State, under the Laws thereof, escaping into another, shall, in Consequence of any Law or Regulation therein, be discharged from such Service or Labour, but shall be delivered up on Claim of the Party to whom such Service or Labour may be due.

Section 3. New States may be admitted by the Congress into this Union; but no new State shall be formed or erected within the Jurisdiction of any other State; nor any State be formed by the Junction of two or more States, or parts of States, without the Consent of the Legislatures of the States concerned as well as of the Congress.

The Congress shall have Power to dispose of and make all needful Rules and Regulations respecting the Territory or other Property belonging to the United States; and nothing in this Constitution shall be so construed as to Prejudice any Claims of the United States, or of any particular State.

Section 4. The United States shall guarantee to every State in this Union a Republican Form of Government, and shall protect each of them against Invasion; and on Application of the Legislature, or of the Executive (when the Legislature cannot be convened) against domestic Violence.

Article v

The Congress, whenever two-thirds of both Houses shall deem it necessary, shall propose Amendments to this Constitution, or, on the Application of the Legislatures of two-thirds of the several States, shall call a Convention for proposing Amendments, which, in either Case, shall be valid to all Intents and Purposes, as part of this Constitution, when ratified by the Legislatures of three-fourths of the several States, or by Conventions in three-fourths thereof, as the one or the other Mode of Ratification may be proposed by the Congress; Provided that no Amendment which may be made prior to the Year One thousand eight hundred and eight shall in any Manner affect the first and fourth Clauses in the Ninth Section of the first Article, and that no State without its Consent, shall be deprived of its equal Suffrage in the Senate.

Article vi

All Debts contracted and Engagements entered into, before the Adoption of this Constitution shall be as valid against the United States under this Constitution, as under the Confederation.

This Constitution, and the Laws of the United States which shall be made in Pursuance thereof, and all Treaties made, or which shall be made, under the Authority of the United States, shall be the supreme Law of the Land, and the Judges in every State shall be bound thereby, any Thing in the Constitution or Laws of any State to the Contrary notwithstanding.

The Senators and Representatives before mentioned, and the Members of the several State Legislatures, and all executive and judicial Officers, both of the United States and of the several States, shall be bound by Oath or Affirmation, to support this Constitution; but no religious Test shall ever be required as a Qualification to any Office or Public Trust under the United States.

Article vii

The Ratification of the Conventions of nine States shall be sufficient for the Establishment of this Constitution between the States so ratifying the Same.

Done in Convention

by the Unanimous Consent of the States present the Seventeenth Day of September in the Year of our Lord one thousand seven hundred and Eighty seven and of the Independence of the United States of America the Twelfth. In Witness whereof We have hereunto subscribed our Names.

G° WASHINGTON—
Presi[dt] and deputy from Virginia.

NEW HAMPSHIRE

John Langdon — Nicholas Gilman

MASSACHUSETTS

Nathaniel Gorham — Rufus King

CONNECTICUT

Wm. Saml. Johnson — Roger Sherman

NEW YORK

Alexander Hamilton

NEW JERSEY

Wil: Livingston — Wm. Paterson
David Brearley — Jona. Dayton

PENNSYLVANIA

B. Franklin — Thomas Mifflin
Robt. Morris — Geo: Clymer
Tho: Fitzsimons — Jared Ingersoll
James Wilson — Gouv: Morris

DELAWARE

Geo: Read — Gunning Bedford, Jun'r.
John Dickinson — Richard Bassett
Jaco: Broom

MARYLAND

James M'Henry — Dan: of St. Thos. Jenifer
Danl Carroll

VIRGINIA

John Blair — James Madison, Jr.

NORTH CAROLINA

Wm. Blount — Rich'd Dobbs Spaight
Hu. Williamson

SOUTH CAROLINA

J. Rutledge — Charles Cotesworth Pinckney
Charles Pinckney — Pierce Butler

GEORGIA

William Few — Abr. Baldwin

Attest: William Jackson, Secretary

Fifty-five Delegates to the Constitutional Convention

Delegates	*Age on May 14, 1787*	*Principal Occupation*	*Member, Continental Congress*	*Signer, Art. of Confederation*	*Signer, Declaration of Independence*	*In Military Service*	*Signer, Constitution*
EW HAMPSHIRE							
ohn Langdon,							
born June 25, 1741	46					X	X
icholas Gilman,		Merchant	X				
born 1755	32	Soldier	X			X	X
ASSACHUSETTS							
lbridge Gerry,							
born July 17, 1744	43	Merchant	X	X	X		
athaniel Gorham,							
born May 27, 1738	48	Merchant	X				X
ufus King,							
born March 24,							
1755	32	Lawyer	X			X	X
aleb Strong,							
orn Jan. 9, 1745	42	Lawyer					
HODE ISLAND							
(*No appointment*)							
ONNECTICUT							
illiam Samuel							
ohnson, born		Lawyer					
October 7, 1727	59	(Jurist)	X			X	X
oger Sherman,		Lawyer					
orn April 19, 1721	66	(Jurist)	X	X	X		X
liver Ellsworth,							
orn April 29, 1745	42	Jurist	X				
EW YORK							
obert Yates,							
orn Jan. 27, 1738	49	Jurist					
lexander Hamilton,		Lawyer					
orn Jan. 11, 1757	30	(Financier)	X			X	X
hn Lansing, Jr.,							
orn Jan. 30, 1754	33	Jurist	X				

Delegates	*Age on May 14, 1787*	*Principal Occupation*	*Member, Continental Congress*	*Signer, Art. of Confederation*	*Signer, Declaration of Independence*	*In Military Service*	*Signe Const tutio*
NEW JERSEY							
David Brearley, born June 11, 1741	46	Lawyer (Jurist)				X	X
William Churchill Houston, born 1740	47	Lawyer	X			X	
William Paterson, born 1745	42	Lawyer (Jurist)				X	X
William Livingston, born Nov. 30, 1723	63	Lawyer (Editor)	X			X	X
Jonathan Dayton, born Oct. 16, 1760	26	Lawyer	X			X	X
PENNSYLVANIA							
Thomas Mifflin, born 1744	43	Merchant	X			X	X
Robert Morris, born 1734	53	Merchant (Financier)	X	X	X		X
George Clymer, born 1739	48	Merchant	X		X	X	X
Jared Ingersoll, born 1750	37	Lawyer (Jurist)	X				X
Thomas Fitzsimons, born 1741	46	Merchant	X			X	X
James Wilson, born Sept. 14, 1742	44	Lawyer (Jurist)	X		X		X
Gouverneur Morris, born Jan. 31, 1752	35	Lawyer-Businessman	X	X			X
Benjamin Franklin, born Jan. 17, 1706	81	Printer, etc.	X		X		X
DELAWARE							
George Read, born Sept. 18, 1733	54	Lawyer (Jurist)	X		X		X
Gunning S. Bedford, Jr., born 1747	40	Lawyer	X			X	X
John Dickinson, born Nov. 8, 1732	54	Lawyer (Jurist)	X	X		X	X
Richard Bassett, born April 2, 1745	42	Lawyer (Jurist)				X	X

Delegates	*Age on May 14, 1787*	*Principal Occupation*	*Member, Continental Congress*	*Signer, Art. of Confederation*	*Signer, Declaration of Independence*	*In Military Service*	*Signer, Constitution*
Jacob Broom, born 1752	35	Landowner					X
MARYLAND							
James McHenry, born Nov. 16, 1753	33	Surgeon	X			X	X
Daniel of St. Thomas Jenifer, born 1723	64	Lawyer	X				X
Daniel Carroll, born 1756	31	Public service	X	X			X
John Francis Mercer, born May 17, 1759	28	Lawyer	X			X	
Luther Martin, born Feb. 9, 1748	39	Lawyer	X				
VIRGINIA							
George Washington, born Feb. 22, 1732	55	Soldier, Statesman, etc.	X			X	X
Edmund Randolph, born Aug. 10, 1753	33	Lawyer	X			X	
John Blair, born 1732	55	Lawyer					X
James Madison, Jr., born March 16, 1751	36	Lawyer	X				X
George Mason, born 1726	61	Landowner					
George Wythe, born 1726	61	Lawyer (Jurist)	X		X		
James McClurg, born 1746	41	Physician				X	
GEORGIA							
William Few, born June 8, 1748	39	Lawyer (Banker)	X			X	X
Abraham Baldwin, born Nov. 22, 1754	32	Lawyer	X			X	X
William Pierce, born c. 1740	47	Merchant	X			X	
William Houstoun, born 1755	32	Lawyer	X				

Delegates	*Age on May 14, 1787*	*Principal Occupation*	*Member, Continental Congress*	*Signer, Art. of Confederation*	*Signer, Declaration of Independence*	*In Military Service*	*Signer, Constitution*
NORTH CAROLINA							
Alexander Martin, born 1740	47	Merchant-Lawyer	X			X	
William Richardson Davie, born June 20, 1759 (some claim 1756)	27	Lawyer				X	
Richard Dobbs Spaight, born March 25, 1758	29	Public service	X			X	X
William Blount, born March 26, 1749	38	Merchant	X			X	X
Hugh Williamson, born Dec. 5, 1735	51	Physician	X			X	X
SOUTH CAROLINA							
John Rutledge, born 1739	48	Lawyer	X				X
Charles Pinckney, born 1758	29	Lawyer	X			X	X
Charles Cotesworth Pinckney, born Feb. 25, 1746	41	Lawyer				X	X
Pierce Butler, born July 11, 1744	43	Planter	X			X	X

The Marquess of Halifax:

DEFEAT OF THE MODERATE

Charm, elegance, and sardonic wit in politics are assets of more than small value. Though in this age of television the intrusion of the camera seemingly makes it necessary for a public man either to exhibit traits of charm or to become a fallen leader, in truth the well-turned phrase, the pointed jibe, the use of fluency as political asset emerged from the British political arena. The model of the civilized participant in the political thickets may well be an extraordinary Englishman, whose obscurity in the American classroom is a puzzling thing indeed. George Savile, the first marquess of Halifax, could undergo serious study by young political scientists, for he is both proof and refutation of the oft-asserted desire for the leader to be eloquent, witty, all-knowing as well as charming, and well stocked with the right phrase at the proper time, the right riposte at the precise moment.

Halifax was born in Yorkshire on November 11, 1633, and was connected with the great families of Talbot, Wentworth, and Coventry. He served three kings, Charles II, James II, and William of Orange. As a young Yorkshireman, he allied himself with the dashing second duke of Buckingham, then awash with schemes and scheming, and at the height of his power. At that early time, he was developing the traits which were in later life to cast him as an uncommon figure in the highest councils of the land. He was developing also other qualities which were, soon and often, to be his undoing as well as his shield.

The diarist John Evelyn recounts a visit by the twenty-nine-year-old Savile. "Sir George," wrote Evelyn, "is a witty gentleman, if not a little too prompt and daring." His biographer, Miss H. C. Foxcroft, describes his strong taste for religious speculation. She said he had "an acute skeptical intellect" and a "keen eye for the failing of the clergy, as well as a sarcastically unbridled tongue." Halifax simply could not resist producing an epigram, no matter how profane or pungent. His aphorisms came not so much from his conviction as from an irrepressible urge to rid himself of a piece of wit that struggled to pop out. Will Durant painted Halifax as "occasionally unscrupulous, always eloquent, and perilously witty."

Halifax regarded office seekers, crowding the corridors with each change of officeholder, as a foul by-product of freedom. But he never intended that any of these wayfarers should be clothed in real responsibility. He recalled that the cackling of frightened sacred geese awakened the Roman garrison in 390 B.C. and saved the capital from the Celts. "Rome was saved by geese," was his wry comment, "but I do not remember that these geese were made consuls."

He accused Lord Rochester, first lord of the Treasury, of stealing public monies. As a result of the inquiry, the first lord was removed and appointed to the less remunerative but more dignified post of lord president. "I have seen people kicked downstairs," observed Halifax, "but my Lord Rochester is the first person I ever saw kicked upstairs." And thus a quotation was born.

When the Tories groused about his going over to the Whigs, Halifax answered: "Ignorance maketh most men go into a party, and shame keepeth them from getting out of it." To a dissident group flailing him in an argument, Halifax said: "Nothing has an uglier look to us than reason, when it is not on our side." Once, in an aside that might have been aimed at himself, he said: "He that leaves nothing to chance will do few things ill, but he will do very few things." And then, as if still to pin down his own voids: "A man may dwell so long upon a thought, that it may take him prisoner."

When the seeds of war and rebellion were being flung through the English countryside, Halifax commented: "In an unreasonable age, a man's reason let loose would undo him." He was a shrewd observer of the court scene, the shuffle and the jostle of power seekers and power brokers. He wrote: "It is safer for a prince to judge of men by what they do to one another, than what they do to him." He took a dim view of civil war, for the rousements of the mob disenchanted his rational intellect. "When the people contend for their liberty," he wrote, "they seldom get anything by their victory but new masters."

Halifax was not affectionate of the instincts of the people. "If none were to have liberty but those who understand what it is, there would not be many freed men in the world," he said. But he also understood how force and power operated, and that those who proclaimed their insistence that the citizen be free did not want the liberty to be total. "Power is so apt to be insolent, and liberty to be saucy, that they are seldom on good terms." He was neither the best nor the worst of husbands, but he had some humor about it: "A wife is to thank God her husband has faults. A husband without faults is a dangerous observer."

In his *History,* Gilbert Burnet says: "Halifax passed for a bold and determined atheist, though he often protested to me that he was not one, and said he could not swallow down everything that divines imposed on the world, but he was a Christian in submission. He believed as much as he could, and he hoped God would not lay it to his charge if he could not take into his belief things that would burst him." Halifax had little use for noisy clerics or loud declaimers of faith. He wrote: "Men pretend to serve Almighty God who doth not need it, but make use of Him because they need Him."

In the Restoration, the state business of Charles II was handled by a quintet, whose names gave birth to a splendid word which to this moment is still full of sinister odor: Sir Thomas Clifford, the earl of Arlington, the duke of Buckingham, Lord Ashley, and the earl of Lauderdale—whose last-name initials produced the word *cabal*. This also was the era when famous labels for two political parties came into vogue, and then into history. In Scotland, a persecuted band of Presbyterian zealots, most numerous in the western Lowlands, took up arms against Charles I. They were called Whiggamores. Thus, the group in England disposed to oppose the court and to treat nonconformist Protestants with some indulgence were called Whigs. Meanwhile, the bogs of Ireland gave refuge to a gang of popish outlaws who preyed on Protestant passers-by. Their name was given to the political faction who refused to bar a Roman Catholic prince from the throne. They were called Tories.

Halifax never was a rigid party man, and at various times he brought down on his head the outrages, as well as the anger, of both Tory and Whig. When, on one occasion, some of his enemies flayed him for deserting the Tories, he answered in a still-famous pamphlet, *The Character of a Trimmer*. This one passage summed him up best:

> The innocent word Trimmer signified no more than this, that if men are together in a boat and one part of the company would weight it down on one side, another would make it lean as much to the contrary; it happens there is a third opinion, of those who conceive it would do as well if the boat were even.

The label "Trimmer" stuck to him, and was used by some as epithet and others as laurel. It depended, of course, on who was doing what to whom.

Though distinguished by his antipapal views, Halifax's finest moment came in 1680 in debate over the lamentable and devouring Exclusion Bill, whereby any future prince of Catholic faith would be barred from the throne. This bill was aimed specifically at James. The House of Commons, with its preponderance of Whigs, had passed the bill. The King was cornered, his allies had deserted him, even his cabinet, Sunderland, Godolphin, Shaftesbury, and Essex were arrayed for the bill. Only Halifax, the skeptic, the maligner of the clergy, whom James, duke of York, had once described with some rasp as "an atheist who had no bowels"—only Halifax stood forth in the House of Lords to stop the bill. Macaulay wrote: "Old men who lived to admire the eloquence of Pulteney in its meridian, and that of Pitt in its splendid dawn still murmured that they had heard nothing like the great speeches of Lord Halifax on the Exclusion Bill." The bill was rejected.

When Parliament later determined how the colony of Massachusetts was to be governed, it was Halifax who animated the great theme of representative government. Had his argument carried, the Revolutionary War might never have been fought, for Halifax exposed the raw nerve of what later became an intolerable pain to the colonists. It is ridiculous, said Halifax, to think that a population sprung from English stock would long suffer to be deprived of English institutions. He was swept aside, his fears regarded as follies, and the germ of revolution at that moment began to prosper.

While Halifax did not misunderstand the sensitive human spirit, he had a more reasonable fault. He tended to give such spacious view to both sides of a question that he waited—that awful, brief, hesitant waiting—beyond the crucial instant in which, if the job is to be done, it must be done now, quickly. The man of political genius knows by instinct, like the visceral reflex of a jungle animal, when the time has come, and at that instant he springs, for he knows it is perilous to delay. Halifax understood the peril of dalliance but was rooted in his reluctance to decide.

In those early days, politics dealt sometimes with crowds, and Halifax recoiled from crowds. He was not a public rostrum man, and the slap of hand against hand in political campaigning would have sent him fleeing to his home in terror. Once he wrote: "There is an accumulative cruelty in a number of men, though none in particular are ill-natured . . . the angry buzz of a multitude is one of the bloodiest noises in the world."

He was much like the nineteenth-century aristocrat, Lord Rosebery, who in 1894 became the first prime minister in many years who had not served in the House of Commons. Rosebery's Etonian tutor once said of him, "He sought the palm without the dust," and Professor Goldwin Smith remarked to Churchill: "Rosebery feels about democracy as he were holding a wolf by the ears." Churchill summed up Halifax's and Rosebery's defect: "Whatever one may think about democratic government it is just as well to have practical experience of its rough and slatternly foundations."

But the qualities in Halifax most pertinent for today are his modern outlook toward ancient problems, the fluid clarity of his aphorisms, and the way he played the role of the intellectual as a brave and reasonable leader who does not rejoice so much in lost causes as he does in just triumphs. That which guided him in the seventeenth century is very alive in the twentieth.

The principles and programs which he advocated three hundred years ago were as ill-favored by his contemporaries as they are in good season today. He believed in compulsory education at public cost. He advocated religious toleration, even though he saw grave problems in the attitude then of the Roman church. He knew that Ireland had reasonable grievances which cried out for redress. His views on the American colonies were the very policies which would have made a rebellion unnecessary. He recognized, in that early day, the importance of political organization, as contrasted to mere numbers. He repeatedly declared the need for a balance of powers between Crown and Parliament, between executive and legislative. He never hesitated to be in the front rank of parliamentary battles for the enlarging of individual liberty. He fought for habeas corpus and against its repeal. He opposed Danby's testing bill, which would have required members of both houses and those holding office to swear that it was a crime to take up arms against the king for any reason whatsoever, as well as altered the arrangement between church and state. His policy of "trimming," balancing opposing forces, was forever his policy and always his principle.

His policy of moderation cost him enduring support from both Tory and Whig. He was accused of treachery by every group which wanted to enlist his formidable talents on its side, and denounced by other groups who feared he would join the opposition. Many times, Halifax was flung into a crossfire, with opposite sides attacking him at once—liberal Whigs reviling him, conservative Tories sneering at him. Like a shuttlecock in a badminton game, Halifax was forced too often to engage in beating back simultaneous attacks, placating none, incensing all.

He was a total man of politics, but politics did not encircle him totally. He was elected a Fellow of the Royal Society, and participated in hydraulic experiments as well as writing about the epic work in transfusion of blood. "The government of the world," he said, "is a great thing, but it is a very coarse one, too, compared with the fineness of speculative knowledge."

He was never agreeable to believing a king. He accounted the ornaments of power so blindingly beautiful to monarchs that their word was of small substance. In his *Letter to a Dissenter* (1687), he warned the nonconformists that there was a clear and present danger in putting their trust in a king's promises to be tolerant. However, if he discounted the pledge of a king, he gave full measure to the plague of a war.

His last great task was, in his trimming tradition, to accommodate the reign of William and Mary. William, like Halifax, wanted to "trim," to reconcile, and Halifax became his instrument. But Halifax grew tired. There was still heat and abrasion in the land, and, as usual, Halifax was in the center, counseling all to diminish their fever, and their fervor. But he had no base of support. The Whigs hated him and the Tories did not love him. He surrendered the Privy Seal, resigned, and six years later was dead at the age of sixty-one.

The shame and waste of Halifax is his lack of durable impress on the great issues of his time. There is no doubt of his ability nor of the passion and persuasion with which he invested any cause that commanded his dedication. But he wrote on the wind, leaving no imprint, the government resisting the embrace of his moderating mind, and the nation deaf to his counsel. He may have believed that what he advocated and what he pursued were beyond the ken of his time. And he may have grown weary of trying to balance opposing and, too frequently, irreconcilable forces.

To be a moderating force in times of change and stress is a shamefully difficult task. In our modern society the rational voice is lost, a distant echo among the din and clang of demagogues, militants, and spoilers. Today, one need only declare his intent to kill someone, or destroy something, and he is instantly displayed on every news show in the country, miraculously transformed into a celebrity; and, if the process is repeated enough times, darkened each time by some new infusion of venom, one can become a national figure, recognizable on every street corner, and sought out for a presence on the late-night talk shows.

The rational man quickly understands that he has no rostrum from which he can preach restraint. Restraint by its very nature is barred from the collection of news each day, simply because restraint is not news. Visibility of one's views is urgent in today's society, because a leader must reach the people if he is to be heard and listened to; and yet to reach the people he must be engulfed in a torrent so rapid and so confused that only a loud snarl or the sound and flash of an unsheathed saber can capture the news and the attention of the public.

This is not to indict the news media. But it is surely a vexing, even sad, summary of the torment of the modern community. The citizen will not lift his eyes or open his ears, seemingly, until he is jolted or frightened or surprised. Perhaps this is what Freud called "intellectual nihilism," wherein all good sense is smashed by the belief that there is no such thing as truth, that it is only the product of our own needs and desires.

The present appears to be an ugly scene which the public, in any age, wants to shuffle off as quickly as possible.

It is also an odd ailment of a free society that its citizens are more apt to revere and long for that which is gone than to support and encourage that which is here. A leader martyred or out of office is invested with wisdom, virtue, and a dynamic presence on a scale which was nowhere publicly to be found when he was in command. There seems to be among a free citizenry impatience with what is and a nostalgia for what was. It is this misadjustment, this collision with a public and parliamentary opinion out of joint with time, that Halifax confronted, suffered, and to which he finally succumbed.

Fretfully, he said: "A very great moment often forgets how much time is lost by repeating things of no use." It was a bitter epigram that may better have served as an epitaph.

Macaulay and His Critics

About Macaulay's *History of England, The Oxford Companion to English Literature* says: ". . . the work, written from a Whig and Protestant point of view, is criticized as showing partiality. Nevertheless, it was, and remains, extremely popular. . . ." Thus *The Oxford Companion* demonstrates the same kind of cool certitude that Lord Melbourne and other critics found so sour in Macaulay. (Lord Melbourne is alleged to have said: "I wish I were as sure of any one thing as Macaulay is of everything.") Too many people have a faint aroma of deprecation when they look at a man like Macaulay. They pat him on the head, nod patronizingly at his inventiveness of phrase, and even mildly approve of his eloquence. And then they put him in the attic with old Japanese screens, a Franklin stove, and some volumes of James Branch Cabell.

The dismemberment of Macaulay begins with recalling him as a readable historian and ends with the dismissal of him as a credible one. The axes that fall on Macaulay are veiled behind a curtain of respect. William Henry Chamberlin describes his style as "fluent, vivid, and colorful." And he quietly slits the jugular with this sharp edge: "He was a magnificent middlebrow, opening up . . . vistas of history . . . without making undue demands" on the reader.

Even Woodrow Wilson, whose stern Calvinism might have found larger rapport with Macaulay, took him on. Mainly to reveal Walter Bagehot as the complete and accurate stylist, Wilson reproved Macaulay for his lucidity of expression, and testified that reading Macaulay excited the mind and spirit but afterward there was a great letdown.

The critics insist that Francis Bacon's cautionary judgment is sound: "Let there not be a too affectionate study of eloquence, so that men hunt after words more than matter . . . and more after the choiceness of the phrase, and the sweet falling of the clauses. . . ."

Bacon demeaned his own admonition by creating the kind of "round and clean composition" he warned against, much admired in his time and later. For a man who once wrote his uncle, Lord Burghley, that he had taken all knowledge as his province, Bacon's kettle cannot truly call Macaulay's pot black.

But the critics, of all kinds, miss the point. Macaulay's value is not in the assessment put on him by the professional historian. It is the gates he opened to a world of history for uncounted young and old. There are those who seek to learn and long to know, and who need someone to illuminate an ill-lighted part of the world drama for them.

How many people know more about English history than they might if they had not read Macaulay is and will remain unmeasured. Reading the tormented prose of a dull, competent historian, lauded by his colleagues, may be an exercise in discipline. It is not, however, calculated to leave the reader gasping—unless it be for air. There is nothing in the Gospels or canon law or civil statute that compels one to read a book.

Therein lies the point. In order to find out about history, to begin to love it, and enjoy it, and want to know about it, one must read history. That is the first, indispensable step. Thus it is that Macaulay, and others like him—Durant, Catton, Prescott, Churchill, Bagehot, Edith Hamilton, Gibbon, and Schlesinger—make the reading of history sheer fun.

Voltaire put it straight in a lively rejoinder to a historian who had criticized him. This historian had himself just completed a volume, and Voltaire said: "A historian has many duties. Allow me to remind you here of two which are of some importance. The first is not to slander, and the second is not to bore. I can excuse you for neglect of the first because few will read you. I cannot, however, forgive you for neglecting the second, for I was forced to read you."

For uncounted millions of the untaught who awaken at the stirrings of sound and melody, who rise, enlivened, at the unfolding of the human drama, there needs to be a Macaulay who touches them and makes them eager and frequent visitors into the world of books.

No one has excelled him in the onward rush and sweep of vowels given voice. Hear this indictment of James Ferguson, Scot and, according to Macaulay, a scoundrel: "Violent, malignant, regardless of truth, insensible to shame, insatiable of notoriety, delighting in intrigue, in tumult, in mischief for its own sake, he toiled during many years in the darkest mines of fiction."

John Wildman, an antimonarchist and former soldier now turned to incursions against the government, was etched unforgettably in two short sentences: "But with Wildman's fanaticism was joined a tender care for his own safety. He had a wonderful skill in grazing the edge of treason."

Macaulay had a gift, too, for the brief and the terse, in which all that needed to be said was said: "Many were kept steady to their old creed by conscience, and many by shame."

He spread on an open board an ample view of England's Charles II:

> He was so far humane that it was highly disagreeable to him to see [his subjects'] sufferings or to hear their complaints. This however is a sort of humanity which, though amiable and laudable in a private man whose power to help or hurt is bounded by a narrow circle, has in princes often been rather a vice than a virtue. No man is fit to govern great societies who hesitates

about disobliging the few who have access to him for the sake of the many whom he will never see.

He set forth in implacable terms the Whig view of government:

> While the chief magistrate governs according to law, he ought to be obeyed and reverenced; that when he violates the law, he ought to be withstood; and that, when he violates the law grossly, systematically and pertinaciously, he ought to be deposed.

And he had the magic taste for the targeted anecdote. James II's son-in-law was one of the dullest royal princelings ever to be revealed to any court anywhere in Western civilization. Charles II's estimate of him was recorded by Macaulay: "I have tried Prince George sober, and I have tried him drunk; and drunk or sober, there is nothing in him."

Nineteen nobles and prelates called on James II in the dying hours of his reign, before his flight, and urged the stubborn monarch to call a free Parliament. The king scorned them, and Macaulay recorded this dialogue:

> "You would be better employed in teaching them how to obey than in teaching me how to govern," said the King. He was much incensed against his nephew Grafton, whose signature stood next to that of Sancroft, and said to the young man with great asperity, "You know nothing about religion; you care nothing about it; and yet, forsooth, you pretend to have a conscience."
>
> "It is true, sir," answered Grafton, with impudent frankness, "that I have very little conscience, but I belong to a party which has a great deal."

This is the case to be made for Macaulay. His history is heavy with words, but the words are never heavy. It makes little difference that Macaulay was adrift with some predictions. Aristotle has long been proved wrong on many of his conclusions, but that does not lessen today's taste for what he wrote. It is of small moment that Macaulay was helplessly Protestant in his theology or hopelessly Whig in his politics. That, too, misses the point.

What is important, and of more than substantial moment, is that young people grow up with some sense of history, and some zest for the reading of it. When one has been introduced to a cadence and roll, a sublime instinct for the marriage of ideas and language that has all the properties of a great suspenseful drama, he may well choose to venture further, where he will meet others whose lines may drop deeper and whose insights may or may not be more perceptive. He will be ready then to be slightly bored, and equipped to bear it, for at least he has the zest of history in his veins.

The one problem about reading Macaulay may be described as being akin to smoking pot. The carpentry of the sentences—the way the words fit together, no uneven edges, all of a piece—gives the reader a kind of floating assurance that he can do it, too.

Alas, he can't.

Perhaps this is one reason why those who cannot duplicate him deprecate him. Moreover, it is fashionable to scorn and square to praise. The ages accept the clout and dismiss the joy. Few critics who glory in a talent ever reside in an anthology, and few epigrams that summarize a eulogy ever find lodging in Bartlett's.

At times, one almost believes that a closed society exists among those who place literary values on what we read. There is abundant cause to believe further that the more tangled the prose, the higher the quality of its assessment. In the search for new ways to say old things, some authors, both in fiction and fact, create some paragraphing that is at best puzzling and at worst has all the root origins of Sanskrit harelip. What comes out of the critic's horn is a verdict that declares some unlikely book to be "must reading," "a masterwork," "creation of genius." It is perfectly understandable that many of us are hesitant to interrupt a song of praise about something we think others are more qualified to judge. The result: on coffee tables and book shelves are gleamingly clad volumes which, by oracular pronouncement, are accounted to be quality literature, and which, by common desire, are rarely read—mostly because the books are unreadable. Macaulay never wrote a sentence that wasn't immensely readable.

With the exception of Winston Churchill, there are few who were more critical of Macaulay than Lytton Strachey. (Churchill never forgave Macaulay for what the great man deemed a brutal and unfair attack on his ancestor, Marlborough.) Yet Strachey himself makes the point about history as a narrative, and about the special genius that sets apart those historians who fill their pages with footnotes and despairingly difficult prose from those who describe and interpret with the artist's sensitive touch. Strachey marks Macaulay as stuffy, blindly partisan to the Macaulay point of view, and catalogues him as being possessed of a certain crudity, even ingenious and complacent.

But, says Strachey, in a burst of candor, "the weaknesses are obvious and the strength, suitably enough, is obvious too. History is primarily a narrative and in power of narration no one has ever surpassed Macaulay. In that he is a genius. When it comes to telling a story, his faults disappear, or change into virtues. Every word is valuable; there is no hesitation, no confusion, and no waste. . . . The rhetoric of the style, from being the ornament of platitude, becomes the servant of excitement."

We often forget that Macaulay was not merely an observer. He was in the political pit, a member of Parliament for fourteen years. On April 15, 1830, he delivered his maiden speech in support of a bill for the removal of Jewish disabilities. Then, on March 2, 1831, at the age of thirty-one, Macaulay rose in the Commons, and flung himself into the bitter struggle over the Reform Bill. His speech that evening was a remarkable testament of fluency and logic. He ended it in a fiery outbreak that caused, as they say in the records, "some agitation."

> Renew the youth of state. Save property, divided against itself. Save the multitude, endangered by its own ungovernable passions. Save the aristocracy, endangered by its own unpopular power. Save the greatest, and fairest, and most highly civilized community that ever existed from calamities which may in a few days sweep away all the rich heritage of so many ages of wisdom and glory. The danger is terrible. The time is short. If this bill should be rejected, I pray to God that none of those who concur in rejecting it may ever remember their votes with unavailing remorse amidst the wreck of laws, the confusion of ranks, the spoliation of property, and the dissolution of social order.

When he sat down, we are told by his nephew, Sir George Otto Trevelyan, "The Speaker sent for him and told him that in all his prolonged experience he had never seen the House in such a state of excitement."

Which is the state of one who reads Macaulay's *History and Essays.*

BIBLIOGRAPHY

Adams, Henry. *John Randolph*. Boston: Houghton Mifflin Company, 1883.

Anderson, Fulton Henry. *Francis Bacon: His Career and His Thought*. Los Angeles: University of Southern California Press, 1962.

Bacon, Francis. *Selected Writings of Francis Bacon*. New York: Modern Library, 1955.

Bacon, Francis. *Bacon's Essays, with Annotations by Richard Whately, and Notes and Glossarial Index by Franklin Fiske Heard*. Boston: Lee and Shepard, 1868.

Bagehot, Walter. *The Collected Works of Walter Bagehot*. Edited by Norman St. John-Stevas. Cambridge: Harvard University Press, 1965.

Blake, Robert. *Disraeli*. London: Eyre & Spottiswoode Ltd., 1966.

Bowen, Catherine Drinker. *Francis Bacon: The Temper of A Man*. Boston: Little, Brown and Company, 1963.

Bowen, Catherine Drinker. *John Adams and the American Revolution*. Boston: Little, Brown and Company, 1950.

Bowen, Catherine Drinker. *Miracle at Philadelphia*. Boston: Little, Brown and Company, 1966.

Bowers, Claude. *Jefferson and Hamilton*. Boston and New York: Houghton Mifflin Company, 1933.

Bowers, Claude. *Jefferson in Power*. Boston: Houghton Mifflin Company, 1936.

Brant, Irving. *The Bill of Rights*. Indianapolis: Bobbs-Merrill, Inc., 1965.

Bright, Robert S. *The Hamlet of American Politics*. Address during Commencement at College of William and Mary, Williamsburg, Va., 1908.

Cooke, J. E. (ed.). *The Federalist*. Middletown, Conn.: Wesleyan University Press, 1961.

Costain, Thomas B. *The Magnificent Century*. Garden City, N.Y.: Doubleday & Company, Inc., 1962.

Costain, Thomas B. *The Three Edwards*. Garden City, N.Y.: Doubleday & Company, Inc., 1962.

Coventry, Sir W. *The Character of a Trimmer*, 2nd ed. London: R. Baldwin, 1689.

Dabney, Richard Heath. *John Randolph, a Character Sketch*. Milwaukee: H. G. Campbell Publishing Co., 1903.

Disraeli, Benjamin. *Wit and Wisdom of Benjamin Disraeli, Earl of Beaconsfield*. New York: D. Appleton & Company, 1881.

Dodd, Alfred. *Francis Bacon's Personal Life Story*. London and New York: Rider & Co., 1949.

Dodd, Alfred. *The Martyrdom of Francis Bacon; Being A Close Inquiry into the Circumstances Surrounding His "Fall" as Lord Chancellor*. London and New York: Rider & Co., 1945.

Durant, Will, and Ariel Durant. *The Age of Louis XIV*. New York: Simon & Schuster, Inc., 1963.

Durant, Will. *Rousseau and Revolution*. New York: Simon & Schuster, Inc., 1967.

Durant, Will. *The Story of Philosophy*. New York: Simon & Schuster, Inc., 1933.

Durant, Will. *The Age of Voltaire*. New York: Simon & Schuster, Inc., 1965.

Durant, Will. *The Age of Faith*. New York: Simon & Schuster. Inc., 1950.

Durant, Will, and Ariel Durant. *The Lessons of History*. New York: Simon & Schuster, Inc., 1968.

Farrand, Max. *The Records of the Federal Convention of 1787*. New Haven, Conn.: Yale University Press, 1966. Four volumes.

Foxcroft, Helen Charlotte. *A Character of a Trimmer; Being a Short Life of the First Marquis of Halifax*. Cambridge, England: The University Press, 1946.

Foxcroft, Helen Charlotte. *The Life and Letters of Sir George Savile, first marquis of Halifax*. London and New York: Longmans, Green, & Co., 1898.

Fraser, Sir William A. *Disraeli and His Day*, 2nd ed. London: K. Paul, Trench, Trubner, & Co., Ltd., 1891.

Hamilton, Edith. *The Greek Way*. New York: W. W. Norton & Company, 1964.

Harris, Leon A. *The Fine Art of Political Wit*. New York: E. P. Dutton & Co., 1964.

James, Marquis. *The Life of Andrew Jackson*. Indianapolis: Bobbs-Merrill, Inc., 1938.

Johnson, Gerald W. *Randolph of Roanoke: A Political Fantastic*. New York: Minton, Balch, & Company, 1929.

Kelly, Amy. *Eleanor of Aquitaine and the Four Kings*. Cambridge, Mass.: Harvard University Press, 1950.

Kirk, Russell. *Randolph of Roanoke; a Study in Conservative Thought*. Chicago: Henry Regnery Co., 1964.

Knowles, C. H. *Simon de Montfort, 1265–1965*. London: The Historical Association, 1965.

Macaulay, Thomas Babington. *History of England*. New York: G. P. Putnam's Sons, 1898.

Madison, James. *The Papers of James Madison*. V. 2, *Debates in Federal Convention May 14, 1787 to August 6, 1787*. V. 3, *Debates in Federal Convention August 7, 1787 to September 17, 1787*. Washington: Langtree & O'Sullivan, 1840.

Maurois, André. *Disraeli, A Picture of the Victorian Age*. Translated by Hamish Miles. New York: The Modern Library, 1942.

Maurois, André. *Voltaire*. Translated by Hamish Miles. New York: D. Appleton and Company, 1932.

Maynell, Wilfred. *The Man Disraeli; An Unconventional Biography*. London: Hutchinson & Co., Ltd., 1927 (revised edition).

Morley, John, Viscount. *Voltaire*. London: The Macmillan Company, 1903.

Murray, David Leslie. *Disraeli*. London: E. Benn, Ltd., 1927.

Neustadt, Richard E. *Presidential Power*. New York: John Wiley & Sons, 1960.

Noyes, Alfred. *Voltaire*. London: Faber and Faber, Ltd., 1939.

Padover, Saul. *The Living U. S. Constitution*. New York: The New American Library, 1968.

Pearson, Hesketh. *Dizzy; the Life and Nature of Benjamin Disraeli, Earl of Beaconsfield.* New York: Harper & Row, 1951.

Peattie, Donald Culross. *Lives of Destiny.* Boston: Houghton Mifflin Company, 1954.

Plutarch. *Lives of the Noble Greeks* and *Lives of the Noble Romans.* Various editions.

Rossiter, Clinton. *1787: The Grand Convention.* New York: The Macmillan Company, 1966.

Schachner, Nathan. *Thomas Jefferson, A Biography.* Vols. I & II. New York: Appleton-Century-Crofts, Inc., 1951.

Schlesinger, Arthur. *A Thousand Days.* Boston: Houghton Mifflin Company, 1965.

Standish, Frank Hall. *The Life of Voltaire.* London: Printed for J. Andrews, 1821.

Torrey, Norman Lewis. *The Spirit of Voltaire.* New York: Columbia University Press, 1938.

Trevelyan, George Otto. *Life and Letters of Lord Macaulay.* Detroit: Belford Brothers, 1876.

Wellman, Paul. *The House Divides.* Garden City, N.Y.: Doubleday & Company, Inc., 1966.

White, Theodore. *The Making of the President.* New York: Atheneum, 1968.

About the Author

Jack Valenti, despite vigorous activity in business, political, and international affairs, is no occasional weekend author. Writing has been his passion since school and university days in Houston, Texas, and at Harvard, through his years in the White House as Special Assistant to President Johnson, and to the moment as President of the Motion Picture Association of America.

His preference in writing, as in reading, is catholic. He finds an absorbing fascination "with extraordinary men" and with difficult issues in history which are not dissimilar to our own today.

"Get Jack Valenti!" said the man who had just become the 36th President of the United States on that dark day in Dallas, November 22, 1963. Valenti boarded Air Force One for Washington to become Special Assistant to Lyndon Baines Johnson, the man he had long admired as friend, as United States Senator, as the Vice President.

Valenti remained at President Johnson's side until the spring of 1966, when he became president of the Motion Picture Association.

Valenti, who was born in Houston, is a graduate of the University of Houston and of Harvard University's Graduate School of Business Administration. During World War II he flew 51 combat missions with the U. S. 12th Air Force in Italy for which he won the Distinguished Flying Cross. He is married to the former Mary Margaret Wiley. They have three young children, two daughters and a son, and their home is in Washington, D. C.